MODERN HUMANITIES RESEARCH ASSOCIATION
NEW TRANSLATIONS
VOLUME 16

THE EYES

BY

PABLO MESSIEZ

MODERN HUMANITIES RESEARCH ASSOCIATION
NEW TRANSLATIONS

The guiding principle of this series is to publish new translations into English of important works that have been hitherto imperfectly translated or that are entirely untranslated. The work to be translated or re-translated should be aesthetically or intellectually important. Proposals for new entries in the series are welcome. The proposal should cover such issues as copyright and, where relevant, an account of the faults of the previous translation/s; it should be accompanied by independent statements from two experts in the field attesting to the significance of the original work (in cases where this is not obvious) and to the desirability of a new or renewed translation.

Translations should be accompanied by a fairly substantial introduction and other, briefer, apparatus: a note on the translation; a select bibliography; a chronology of the author's life and works; and notes to the text.

Titles will be selected by members of the Editorial Board and edited by leading academics.

General Editor
Dr Ann Lewis

Editorial Board
Dr Ann Lewis (French)
Professor Ritchie Robertson (Germanic)
Professor Helena Sanson (Italian)
Professor David Gillespie (Slavonic)
Professor Jonathan Thacker (Spanish)
Professor Cláudia Pazos Alonso (Portuguese)

www.translations.mhra.org.uk

THE EYES
A TELLURIC MELODRAMA

BY

PABLO MESSIEZ

TRANSLATED BY

ALMA PRELEC AND MARÍA BASTIANES

With an Introduction by
MARÍA BASTIANES

And an Interview with Pablo Messiez by
ALMA PRELEC

MODERN HUMANITIES RESEARCH ASSOCIATION
New Translations 16
2024

Published by
The Modern Humanities Research Association
Salisbury House
Station Road
Cambridge CB1 2LA
United Kingdom

© Modern Humanities Research Association, 2024

Alma Prelec and María Bastianes have asserted their right under the Copyright, Designs and Patents Act 1988 to be identified as the author of this work. Parts of this work may be reproduced as permitted under legal provisions for fair dealing (or fair use) for the purposes of research, private study, criticism, or review, or when a relevant collective licensing agreement is in place. All other reproduction requires the written permission of the copyright holder who may be contacted at rights@mhra.org.uk.

First published 2024

ISBN 978-1-83954-631-0 (hardback)
ISBN 978-1-83954-111-7 (paperback)

Typeset in Minion Pro by Allset Journals & Books, Scarborough, UK

CONTENTS

Introduction   1
by María Bastianes

THE EYES   21

Appendix: An Interview with Pablo Messiez   55
by Alma Prelec

Bibliography   65

INTRODUCTION
(María Bastianes)

In an interview that took place in 2018 at the Casa de América in Madrid, Carmen Colino spoke of the origins of an important group of theatre influencers, *tuiteatreros*, of which she was a founding member. The collective was born in 2011 from a spontaneous gathering of Twitter users united by their appreciation of a number of productions staged that season.[1] Among these was *The Eyes* (*Los ojos* in its Spanish original, 2011), a theatrical re-writing of Benito Pérez Galdós's nineteenth-century realist novel *Marianela* by a relative newcomer to the Spanish theatrical scene: the Argentine actor, director and playwright Pablo Messiez. Having trained and worked for many years, primarily as an actor, in the strong so-called Buenos Aires alternative theatre circuit (private small theatres or theatre groups operating outside the profit-driven commercial sector, but also divided from the public or state-funded circuit), Messiez moved to Madrid in 2008. The success of *The Eyes* in Spain bears witness to the influence of the Argentine fringe movement — unique in terms of means of production as well as methods of training and creation — on Spanish audiences and practitioners, especially since 2000, a point to which I will return.[2] Messiez has subsequently become one of the country's most in-demand theatre directors.

But if the Spanish theatre system has learnt to recognise and welcome the formal innovations from the rich Argentine fringe tradition, the same unfortunately cannot be said of the Anglophone world. With a few notable exceptions such as Maria Delgado and Jean Graham Jones, UK and US Hispanists continue to reference Argentine theatre primarily in sociological rather than aesthetic and theatrical terms. Artists are more likely to succeed if they directly address subjects related to Argentina's violent history, as happened recently with Lola Arias's *Campo minado* ('Minefield'), a piece made with veterans from the Falklands/Malvinas War that premiered at the Brighton Festival, before transferring to the Royal Court Theatre and other prestigious

---

[1] Some of its members had participated, as a sort of spokesperson for audiences, in the jury of several editions of the General Society of Authors and Publishers' Max Awards, the most important performing arts prize in Spain.

[2] To mention a recent example: the Spanish company La abducción — whose members included one of the prominent young voices of the contemporary Spanish theatre, Pablo Remón (National Drama Award 2021) — publicly admitted to following the path opened by Argentine creators such as Claudio Tolcachir, Daniel Veronese and Pablo Messiez (see La Vanguardia 2020).

venues. Without denying the quality of Arias's breathtaking work, this kind of preference is regrettable given that it ignores how and why Argentina, particularly Buenos Aires, has become a global theatrical reference point in the twenty-first century within and beyond the Spanish-speaking world.[3] There are, in fact, few cases in the history of Western theatre in which fringe activity has become so nationally and internationally prominent. To convince the reader of this bold claim, I will return to the aesthetic and socio-economic specificities of the Argentine fringe tradition once I have sketched Messiez's personal and professional trajectory.

A final warning: as will become evident, the play contained in this volume was not created as 'dramatic literature', independent from its original production. Messiez conceives his texts as merely 'the words from the plays', as per the title of a published collection of works in which *The Eyes* first appeared (2017). What the actors did with these words — which many times was the play's *raison d'être* — is unfortunately lost in the translation from stage to page.[4] More details are provided about Messiez's double role as dramaturge and director in the interview carried out especially for this edition (see Appendix).

Pablo Messiez's Transatlantic Theatrical Journey

Born in 1974 in Adrogué, a small city of Greater Buenos Aires, Pablo Messiez was attracted to the theatre from a very early age (he was only twelve years old when he began studying acting). At fifteen, he moved to the capital, where he continued his actor and director training under legendary figures of the post-dictatorship alternative circuit such as the director Ricardo Bartís.

Messiez's debut as an actor was in 1993, in the first production by a former classmate, the director Cristian Drut. A big break into professional acting was being cast in the role of the Boy Messenger in Leonor Manso's production of *Waiting for Godot* (1996). The production's success (it was staged at the commercial theatre La Trastienda) gave Messiez privileged access to public and fringe circuits in Buenos Aires, working with directors such as Daniel Suárez

---

[3] In her thesis, Dansilio (2017: 158–66) maps the (geographical and statistical) evolution of the independent circuit. Buenos Aires is currently one of the cities with the most performing arts spaces worldwide (around 374, 25% of the total number in Argentina, according to 2017 data provided on the website of the Cultural Information System from Argentina (see SINCA n.d.). See also the national survey of cultural consumption (Encuesta Nacional de Consumos Culturales 2022) and the recent audience audit of Independent Theatre by the website Alternativa Teatral (Públicos de teatro 2020).

[4] A recording of the 2011 production is available (for free) at the Centre for the Documentation of Performing Arts and Music (CDAEM)'s online platform Teatroteca. The archive of RTVE (the Spanish Radio and Television Corporation) also features a radio interview with Messiez and the actor Oscar Velado on the production (see La Caja del Apuntador 2011).

Marzal, Rubén Szuchmacher and Daniel Veronese. The latter played a key albeit indirect role in Messiez's later trajectory as a director in Spain.

In 2004 Messiez played Natasha in *Un hombre que se ahoga* ('A Man Who Drowns'), a version of *Three Sisters* and the first of Veronese's influential trilogy reimagining Chekhov's plays. Produced on the fringe circuit, *Un hombre que se ahoga* toured several countries, among them Spain, where it was seen first at Gerona's 2006 Temporada Alta festival and, later, at Madrid's National Drama Centre (CDN). The following year it was staged at the Teatre Lliure in Barcelona, one of the most prestigious venues in Catalonia. This jump from festivals to theatre programming did not come about by chance. The exchange between the Argentine fringe circuit and Spanish theatre was already evident by the end of the 1980s, with the arrival of groups such as Ricardo Bartís's Sportivo Teatral and, later, the company Periférico de Objetos — the Ibero American Theatre Festival of Cádiz (created in 1985), and the Sala Beckett in Barcelona (founded in 1989) played major roles in this process. However, since 2002 it has increased exponentially (see Salvatierra Capdevila 2013; Ramírez de Haro 2006: 212).[5]

Messiez's Spanish debut would have an important impact on his personal and professional life. In 2008 he moved to Madrid, 'trying to salvage a relationship that was falling apart' (see p. 55). Concerned with the limitations his accent might impose on his work as an actor, Messiez decided to focus on direction, a pathway he had already begun in Buenos Aires with *Antes* ('Before'), a free adaptation of Carson McCullers's novel *The Member of the Wedding* (1946), which premiered at the fringe theatre Camarín de las Musas in 2007.

Messiez's directorial debut in Spain was *Muda* ('Mute', 2010), a personal creation also influenced by Carson McCullers (the piece took inspiration from *The Heart Is a Lonely Hunter*). This initial venture was the result of Messiez's encounter with Fernanda Orazi, a fellow émigré, whom he would go on to cast on multiple occasions. Like Messiez, Orazi had also decided to move to Madrid after a tour (with *Ars Higenica*, directed by another prominent figure of the contemporary Argentine stage, Ciro Zorzoli), and was at the time working as a

---

[5] For instance, from 2006 to 2009 the Argentine playwright and director Javier Daulte was artistic director of the Villarroel Theatre of Barcelona (a venue created in the early seventies during the powerful Spanish independent theatre movement). In 2013 the first Ibero American edition of the Temporada Alta festival was hosted by the fringe Buenos Aires theatre Timbre Cuatro. Timbre Cuatro was founded by another internationally renowned figure of the Argentine stage, Claudio Tolcachir (his *La omisión de la familia Coleman* ('The Omission of the Family Coleman') has been on stage since 2005, touring twenty-two countries); in 2020 Timbre Cuatro opened a second venue in Madrid. It is worth noting that this exchange is primarily centred on the Argentine (and especially Buenos Aires) fringe circuit. According to the partial study carried out by Scherer (2016: 75), 45% of the productions from Buenos Aires that visited Madrid from 2008 to 2015 began their life in the alternative circuit, 20% in the state funded circuit, 20% were a mixture of private and public production, and only 15% were commercial (mainly for-profit) initiatives.

house manager of the Pradillo Theatre, one of Madrid's oldest fringe theatres.[6] After asking Messiez if he had a project in mind that could fit the venue's season, she ended up playing one of the characters in *Muda*, alongside the Spanish actor Óscar Velado and another former member of Ciro Zorzoli's troupe, the Argentine actress Marianela Pensado. The production opened at the Pradillo in January 2010. A year later, Messiez created *The Eyes* (2011) for the same cast, with the addition of actress Violeta Pérez. On this occasion, the production opened on the public circuit, at the Fernán Gómez theatre run by Madrid City Council.

In the subsequent years, Messiez directed productions for the recently created Madrid Fringe Festival (*Las plantas* ('The Plants'), 2012) and the more long-standing Festival de Otoño (*Las palabras* ('The Words'), 2013). For the latter, he made his first incursion into the global canon with a production of Jean Genet's *The Maids* (2012). He also prepared textual material for several hybrid pieces by Losdedae, the company run by prize-winning dancer and choreographer Chevy Muraday. But the major turning point in Messiez's career as a director came with his stage version of Alberto Conejero's *La piedra oscura* ('The Dark Stone', 2015), a co-production by CDN and the private TV, film and theatre producer LaZona (the firm behind the box office cinematic smash *Ocho apellidos vascos / Spanish Affair* (2014)). *La piedra oscura*, a play about the final hours of one of Federico García Lorca's lovers, was the big winner at the annual Max Awards (as noted above, the most prominent performing arts prize in Spain). Messiez himself won in the category for Best Director and had the doors to a number of Madrid's leading theatres opened to him. In 2023 his *La voluntad de creer* ('The Will to Believe') won the Max Award for Best Show, the most prestigious category of the evening. Created prior to this breakthrough moment, *The Eyes* is perhaps best understood as a work of transition in which the modus operandi and influence of Argentina's fringe circuit are clear.

Argentina's Independent Theatre Tradition

The independent model of the Teatro del Pueblo

The success of Argentina's contemporary alternative circuit is the continuation of a long-standing independent (in relation to the for-profit and state funded circuits) tradition of producing and thinking about theatre. The foundation of the Teatro del Pueblo ('Theatre of the People') by writer and journalist Leónidas Barletta in 1930 is generally credited as the starting point for this tradition (see Fukelman 2017). Created with an overtly leftist agenda (Barletta had affiliations

---

[6] The venue opened its doors in the nineties and was linked to the beginnings on stage of some of the most internationally renowned figures of Spanish contemporary performance and performing arts, such as Rodrigo García and La Ribot.

with the Communist Party) at a time of heightened political tension (a couple of months after a coup had paved the way for Argentina's first dictatorship of the twentieth century), the Teatro del Pueblo was born with a double mission: to provide a space for theatrical experimentation and to educate the masses. It thereby combined two important late nineteenth-century European traditions: the art and popular theatre movements. The venture began in a converted dairy on the bustling Corrientes Avenue (the street was and still is a symbol of the theatrical and cultural life of the city of Buenos Aires) and remained in small venues until it came to an end in 1975, following Barletta's death and shortly before the establishment of Argentina's most recent dictatorship, in 1976. According to Larra (1978: 81–83), the Teatro del Pueblo was committed to providing accessible (or even free) tickets, and resisted public and private funding. Members were instructed not to subsidise their labour by working in the commercial for-profit circuit, and were instead encouraged to take non-theatrical jobs to pay the bills.

Even allowing for certain contradictions (not least the weight of Barletta's decisions and opinions in a purportedly collective endeavour (see Fukelman 2017)), the Teatro del Pueblo provided a model for future independent initiatives in three key respects: commitment to theatrical and political activism; privileging artistic over commercial considerations; and replacing the traditional hierarchies of an actor-manager company with an associative horizontal model. This third factor favoured role fluidity, with practitioners taking on other managerial and technical roles (e.g. selling tickets, cleaning). From the outset, the Teatro del Pueblo was committed also to supporting those local playwrights who sought to create 'un teatro nacional en consonancia con nuestros problemas y nuestra sensibilidad' ('a national theatre that could connect with our problems and tastes').[7] These are the words of Roberto Arlt (1942), one of Argentina's most admired cult novelists (praised by the likes of Jorge Luis Borges, Roberto Bolaño and César Aira), speaking in his lesser-known capacity of playwright. He was, in fact, the most important author related to the Teatro del Pueblo.

The professional turn: Independent becomes alternative

The 1950s saw important changes in the independent circuit. Leaving behind the Teatro del Pueblo's initial aversion to profit in any guise, other groups adopted a co-operative model as they strove for professionalisation and to be less hermetically sealed from commercial or subsidised theatre. In 1968 fringe

---

[7] All translations are my own. While many times dealing with local problems, such as immigration, the two native popular trends of Argentine theatre, the *sainete criollo* and the *grotesco criollo*, were perceived as shallow and formulaic (Pellettieri 2006: 70). We must bear in mind that, according to the periodisation proposed by Pellettieri (2003: 20), the emergence of an Argentine theatrical system began late, with the staging in 1884 of *Juan Moreira* and the appearance of the *gauchesco* drama.

activity was belatedly incorporated into Argentina's employment and labour legislation. Small theatre groups could, for the purposes of a single project, become Sociedades Accidentales de Trabajo para Cooperativas de Teatro ('Provisional Companies for Theatre Cooperatives'). This legal formula involved seed funding from external investors, constituting a compromise with market forces and the point of departure for the current Argentine alternative or fringe circuit.

In line with this professionalization, a growing concern for providing better actor training resulted in the creation of in-house private studios; these had firmly taken root as the dominant model by the late 1950s (see Pellettieri 2003: 101–08; Tirri 1973: 73). Run, in general, by a renowned figure from the alternative circuit — teaching their own way of applying a method, many times assisted by their disciples — such private studios have since then proliferated, and are often preferred to state-run schools.[8] For new practitioners, these constitute a space for training and provide opportunities for networking. For established names, they provide employment and business opportunities, given that acting classes are a popular hobby in Argentina (see Bayardo García 1997: 54). With all the necessary disclaimers in place, there is some truth in these words by Battezzati (2019: 6):

> Las obras no importan tanto en su éxito en taquilla y con respecto al público en general como en lo que contribuyen a dar un nombre al director, que este puede capitalizar a partir de las clases que imparte. Dicho de otro modo, el teatro alternativo puede prescindir de un interés por el mercado de las obras de teatro porque se sostiene a partir del mercado de las clases de actuación.
>
> ('The success of a production is measured by its role in consolidating the name of the director, since this symbolic capital can afterwards be translated into economic capital through classes. In other words, Argentina's fringe theatre can survive without depending on box-office revenues, because it is sustained by acting classes.')

Opening a studio (a space not only to give classes, but also to experiment without the pressure of constant production) is an aspiration for many Argentine practitioners. It was also one of Messiez's aspirations when he started on his professional trajectory in Spain.

---

[8] Conversely, many students that attend state-run institutions train simultaneously at other private schools (see Battezzati 2018: 8). Although more research needs to be done on the subject, this is still probably a main difference with the Spanish theatrical system, in which state schools are better regarded (especially the Royal Higher College of Performing Arts, RESAD), and private schools are often seen as a back-up (see Tortosa 2021).

Stanislavsky meets Alberto Olmedo

The institution of the private studios cannot be separated from the arrival to Argentina of Stanislavsky's affective memory technique (in which the actor recalls situations from their own life and projects their feeling onto their characters), later re-appropriated by Lee Strasberg to create the so-called 'Method'. A psychological reading of Stanislavsky (reinforced in the 1970s through Strasberg's visit) soon became the predominant training method for actors in Argentina (see Battezzati 2019: 10–12). A few notable exceptions such as Griselda Gambaro aside, realism also dominated in the dramatic literature of the time.[9] Many practitioners going into exile set up residence in Spain, where they delivered workshops or even opened studios and schools with a clear Stanislavskian bent. Cristina Rota's Sala Mirador, for example, became one of Madrid's most influential private acting schools (its alumni include the Oscar-winner Penélope Cruz (Ciller 2016)).

By the end of the 1980s, however, changes were afoot back in Buenos Aires, as new theatrical languages came to the fore on the alternative circuit, seeking to depart from the hegemony of realist dogma. Among the most cited influences was visual artist Francis Bacon, who sought to 'reinvent realism' (or better, figurative art) through recourse to the un-planned 'inspired accident' (Sylvester 1999: 176, 96, 100).[10] As applied to dramaturgy, new languages challenged traditional structures, relinquishing linear narrative, and introducing instead a tension between the expected and the unexpected (a tension close to the definition of the Freudian uncanny and to the rich Argentine fantastical narrative tradition). Linked to the Baconian idea of 'inspired accident', the use of a 'generative image' (understood as an experience or image that has not been

---

[9] The realist tradition was revitalised during the years of the post-1976 dictatorship, through the desire for a clear unequivocal message (see Pellettieri 2003: 253). One of the major exponents of this political and theatrical activism was the Open Theatre (Teatro Abierto) movement, which was as brief as it was powerful. From 1981 Teatro Abierto challenged the regime's attacks on practitioners by organizing cycles of contemporary plays. As Taylor (1997: 234) explains, 'the idea was that if a whole group of black-listed people worked together, the dictatorship would not be able to clamp down on them all'.

[10] Messiez quotes the Anglo-Irish artist repeatedly in relation to both writing and directing plays. He described to me Sylvester's interviews with Bacon (1999) and Deleuze's book on the British painter (2003) as his principal sources of inspiration when reflecting on the theatrical artistic process. Messiez also complements this reflection on what is (at least rationally) unknown, unforeseen or unexpected with reference to other figures outside the world of theatre, such as the sculptor Eduardo Chillida's *Escritos* and Bresson's *Notes on the Cinematographer*. On his Twitter account, for instance, we can find quotations such as 'Creo que las obras conocidas a priori nacen muertas y que la aventura, al borde de lo desconocido, es la que a veces puede producir el arte' (Chillida 2005: 41) ('I believe that when you know how your piece will be, then this piece is born already dead, only venturing into the unknown can sometimes produce art') or 'Provoke the unexpected. Expect it' (Bresson 1986: 90).

fully consciously processed by the artist's mind (Ferreyra 2019: 15)) became a popular creative device for playwrights from the non-realist tradition (e.g. Ricardo Monti, Mauricio Kartún, Javier Daulte).

In relation to acting, new non-realist languages were included as a means to create rhythm. Key within this trend was the so called *teatro de estados o intensidades* ('theatre of states' or 'theatre of intensities'), which served to make actors more pre-disposed and more able to switch between different emotional states. Looking for a national theatrical style that would not emulate foreign models (in opposition to, say, Argentina's followers of Stanislavsky), the *teatro de estados* returned to popular local acting traditions and their techniques, such as the use of grotesque or even obscene body language, distortion of facial expression, or the use of parody, humour, exaggeration and rambling while speaking (see De Mauro 2011: 389). Scorned by proponents of high culture, such venerable hallmarks of old popular techniques originating in the *sainete criollo* and the so called *género chico* tradition had been relegated to television alongside the commercial theatre and film industries.[11] Actors such as prime-time comedian Alberto Olmedo became reference points, although it is important to note that the *teatro de estados* sought a stylised reappropriation (not restoration) of such popular traditions. The aim was to employ its techniques to create contrast, tension and rhythm, breaking with the conventions of realist theatrical decorum.

A formative influence on Messiez was his training with Ricardo Bartís, a key figure of the *teatro de estados* trend, who, since the 1990s, has been one of Argentina's leading practitioners and teachers (see Rimoldi 2019: 243). Instead of creating a character, in his studio (the Sportivo Teatral) actors train to be affected by what is happening on stage. As Bartís explains (2003: 180): 'un elemento muy fuerte de nuestra estética [es] la idea de aprender a estar, de entrenarnos en estar, no en ser, sino en estar, con gran nivel de conciencia del artificio sin ser coreográficos' ('an important element of our style is to learn to be there, not to be a character, but to be there, conscious all the time that theatre is artifice, but without being choreographic'). Bartís equates theatre to football, and the preparation of an actor to that of an athlete who must learn how to interact with the space and react with speed and elasticity (10). Such a model shifts protagonism from the text to the performer. Bartís's pieces are the result of very long rehearsal periods, a collective process of formative trial and error in which materials are variously selected and discarded. Such an approach requires mutual trust and a strong sense of community (De Mauro 2011: 424). For Bartís (2003: 10),

---

[11] The *género chico* ('short/low theatrical genre') is the generic name used to refer to certain forms of nineteenth-century popular theatre and musical theatre imported from Spain. They are, typically, short comic pieces, featuring simple plots and familiar popular characters that often developed into stock characters.

> uno debe 'creer' en el ensayo. Producir un 'nosotros' aislado del mundo, muy singular, como si fuera un grupo de expedicionarios perdido en el desierto en una búsqueda de una especie de talismán que sería la obra o el espectáculo que durante mucho tiempo no existe o se ve como una quimera, como algo utópico, que uno necesita para darle legalidad a ese deseo y esa voluntad de juntarse y ensayar.

> ('you must have faith during rehearsal. Create a sense of community, an "us" isolated from the rest of the world, very peculiar, akin to being a member of an expedition lost in the desert, looking for some kind of talisman (the production) that for a long time only exists as a pipe-dream, a utopia. It is the pursuit of said utopia that gives meaning to the desire to come together and rehearse.')

From the 1990s onwards, it has been increasingly common for it to be seen as possible and even desirable for practitioners to train in different schools and trends. In conjunction with long periods of rehearsal, this provides one explanation for the much-praised versatility of Argentine actors. In playwright Mauricio Kartún's eloquent synthesis (Peretti 2017):

> En el campo independiente es muy habitual encontrar actores que son capaces de mantener verdad y de pronto quebrar en un juego payasesco y volver a la escena sin perder la verdad de lo que está sucediendo, sin que el espectador sienta que se está haciendo otra cosa que debería entender de otra manera.

> ('It is not uncommon to find actors able to work in a realist style, and all of a sudden, without sacrificing the truth of the endeavour, changing into a clown style and integrating it into to the scene, in such a way that the audience never feels a discontinuity between one thing and the other.')

This organic mixture of realist and non-realist modes is, however, a double-edged sword: texts written for this kind of acting cannot easily be rendered legible for other cultures. Graham Jones (2014: 138) has, for example, documented this phenomenon when translating the playwright Rafael Spregelburd for US audiences, and this is something the reader of the *The Eyes* needs also to be aware of. Before addressing Messiez's text in more detail, however, we need to bring our potted history of alternative theatre production up to date, to encompass the period in which Pablo Messiez came of age.

A small-scale theatre model expands

The last three decades of alternative production have been among the most exciting of Argentina's long independent tradition. Alternative theatre continues to be performed in small (sometimes very small) spaces, often not specifically designed for showcasing theatre (repurposed houses have been used on numerous occasions). One of the most praised features of this format is the proximity of performers and audience, which provides an enviable sense of intimacy. The aforementioned ability to move between roles and the horizontal model of production has produced, over the last three decades, an emblematic figure of Argentina's contemporary alternative scene. The so called *teatrista*, a term coined by Jorge Dubatti (2012: 487–644), refers to practitioners who simultaneously write, direct and sometimes even act in their creations (it is also common for practitioners originally trained as actors to become *teatristas*, as is the case with Messiez). One direct result is a reduced dependence on the established canon, with contemporary plays and radical re-writings of the classics being the norm. Budgetary limitations are eschewed through simple settings, usually formed by household objects the group can easily find — old furniture is, for example, a frequent option. A commitment on the part of the practitioners is manifest through extended periods of (unpaid) rehearsal (much longer than in the commercial or subsidised public circuits).

A 'back-to-basics' model can be seen in the fact that, originally intended to be funded by seed capital from external investors, the aforementioned Provisional Companies for Theatre Cooperatives were (and are still) created and sustained by their members — usually the actors and director, who bear the production and related costs (see Bayardo García 1997: 75–90). Despite this failed business model, a number of internal and external opportunities have helped to fuel the growth of fringe theatre since the end of the 1990s. The creation in 1999 of the Instituto Nacional del Teatro (National Theatre Institute) and Proteatro (a municipal programme by Buenos Aires City Council) added new state funding sources to the already existing funding from the Fondo de las Artes (Arts Fund) (see Rozenholc 2015); although these are still very slim compared to the subsidies or private donations that support theatre in the Global North, and populist president Javier Milei's current austerity plans mean their future is in jeopardy (see Yaccar 2024). A boom in alternative theatre has also been enabled by growing international awareness, with the biannual Buenos Aires International Festival (FIBA), created in 1997, acting as a hub and magnet for foreign producers and programmers.

This new landscape resulted in those practitioners debuting in the alternative circuit in the twenty-first century being more business savvy and possessing greater managerial skills. In line with broader global trends among independent artists (see Rimoldi and Monchietti 2016), Argentine practitioners from the alternative circuit can start a piece without initial funding (to apply for public subsidies, theatre companies need to submit an almost complete project), while having learnt how to attract national and, crucially, international support. Messiez, who worked for festivals in Argentina and Madrid, has often remarked how this cultural management experience helped him forge his own artistic journey (see for instance Romo (2019) and the interview included in the Appendix to this edition, p. 57).

The truth of this claim is easy to document in relation to his arrival in Spain, a country whose thriving independent scene of the last period of the Francoist dictatorship (1939–1975) and the transition to democracy was largely co-opted by the state during the period of PSOE (Spanish Socialist Workers' Party) rule between 1982 and 1996. Spanish practitioners, as a result, became highly dependent on subsidies. The aforementioned actress Fernanda Orazi has, for example, remarked in relation to her experience as a programmer for the Pradillo Theatre that Spanish practitioners would not generally start work on a production prior to securing funding, a pattern of behaviour she attributed to a 'deseo de hacer teatro' ('desire for making theatre') that is less intense than in Argentina, although she also recognises that the precarity of Argentina's alternative system was hardly a model to imitate or export.[12] In the years following the 2008 global financial crisis, which affected Spain in a particularly acute fashion, the situation changed dramatically. With public funding drastically reduced, practitioners needed to adapt to a new state of precarity, a landscape of which Argentine fringe theatre had ample experience.[13]

Post-dictatorship or post-crisis?

Many Argentine scholars place the self-proclaimed National Reorganisation Process (the last of a series of dictatorships that marked the political landscape of Argentina from the thirties on) as the historical event that has had the deepest influence on Argentine theatre, and claim that we are still living in a post-dictatorship theatrical era (the prefix 'post' expresses the idea of a period that comes *after*, but that also is a *consequence* of dictatorship, according to Dubatti (2012: 9)). This hermeneutic has been replicated and often exaggerated in the university systems of the Global North (especially in the English-speaking world — see Rimoldi (2015: 115)). This phenomenon, of course, has an explanation in the way Spanish and Latin American studies are taught (and funded), as part of interdisciplinary macro subjects (modules on memory, violence or trauma in Latin American countries are, for instance, a frequent option in UK university curricula). Yet this produces a reductive image of the cultural production of a

---

[12] See Solé (2021). The fact that this small but flourishing Argentine creative industry (which has, in addition, greatly benefited the cultural image of the country) has at its foundations (and apparently as its only way of functioning) the un(der)paid enthusiasm of those who make it possible has been the object of much recent debate. Indeed, many scholars note how the high symbolic value placed on the independent tradition has been damaging for the rights of its workers (see De Mauro 2018: 136).

[13] Following the Argentine model, many small new spaces opened in those years (such as La casa de la portera ('The House of the Doorwoman'); see Molina 2012), although only a few were able to survive. In this sense, one of the most peculiar creations of Madrid's fringe circuit in this period was Microteatro por dinero ('Micro-theatre for Money'). Founded in a converted brothel, since 2009 Microteatro por dinero has been offering very short productions in a very reduced space, a successful model of production that was subsequently exported to other Spanish and Latin American cities (such as Barcelona, Buenos Aires and Santo Domingo) and even to Miami.

place. If dictatorships are something we must not forget, Latin American cultures have much more to offer that should be remembered. In fact, when questioned about the current success of Argentine theatre, the director and playwright Javier Daulte said that real international consolidation was only possible when practitioners moved away from a stereotypical depiction of the country, embedded in themes such as *desaparecidos* (the forced disappearance of civilians during Argentina's last dictatorship) and tango (interview with Daulte, quoted in Dansilio 2017: 402).

Without wanting to underplay the social, human and theatrical consequences of dictatorship, a strong case can be made that Argentina's economic crisis has had a more significant but much less explored impact on twenty-first-century theatre. For instance, Claudio Tolcachir, one of the most renowned voices of Messiez's generation, claimed that the economic crash was the historical event that most marked his dramaturgy (Cotilla Vaca 2013: 1449). The expansion of the middle classes in Argentina during the twentieth century (particularly marked since the 1950s) was inextricably linked to modernisation and a burgeoning state administration. Urban migration (overwhelmingly from abroad) resulted in an entrenched narrative of effort and (always upward) intergenerational social mobility. Education was the main instrument for social ascent, and culture became an important symbol of class. By the 1980s, 47.4% of the economically active population were classified as middle class, with self-reporting yielding even higher numbers (around 70% of Argentines claimed to belong to this social group (see Kessler and Di Virgilio 2010: 201)). The discrepancy suggests the symbolic power of being middle class in the country's social (and national) imaginaries.

Since then, middle-class stability and prosperity has, however, come under strain, with several waves of impoverishment and unemployment. The 2001 crash (in which a whole family's savings could be and often were wiped out overnight through devaluation) was the most traumatic manifestation of a dysfunctional model. If the 'new poverty' of the early 1990s was experienced by its victims largely with a sense of shame and individual/familial failure, with the 2001 crisis, the impoverished middle classes 'had come out into the open' as a genuine social phenomenon and problem — as Kessler and Di Virgilio state (2010: 216). In a time when all other parameters of social identity had been eroded and dislocated, the middle classes held desperately to culture (Svampa 2005: 154). This provides a compelling explanation for how and why the first decade of the twenty-first century was something of a golden age for theatre in Argentina, especially in Buenos Aires.

An overwhelmingly middle-class art — despite repeated attempts to attract broader popular audiences (the idea of using theatre as a tool to educate those from disadvantaged backgrounds was, for instance, at the origin of the independent movement) — the turn-of-the-century boom in Argentina's alternative circuit was underpinned, albeit not predetermined, by this social identity crisis. From my own experiences of attending the theatre during this period, I can testify to the extent to which it became an art form to reflect on what was happening: confusion and humour were frequently present on stage, employed to confront an equally chaotic reality. The devastating consequences of crisis and social disintegration became a frequent topic in the fringe dramaturgies of the early twenty-first century. From the realist Tolcachir's *La omisión de la familia Coleman* ('The Omission of the Family Coleman', 2005) or *Tercer cuerpo* ('Third Wing', 2008), to the more fragmentary, complex, ludic dramaturgy of *Bizarra* ('Bizarre', 2003) (Rafael Spregelburd's theatrical soap opera in ten episodes), practitioners employed diverse aesthetic strategies to address the crisis. And something similar would happen when crisis crossed the Atlantic.

From crisis to crisis

The consequences of the Argentine economic crisis of 2001 arrived on Spanish stages, especially in the post-2008 crisis context, often through an inverted (*from* instead of *to* Argentina) 'revival' of immigration-themed plays, a topic deeply rooted in Argentina's theatre tradition.[14] For instance, *Un trozo invisible de este mundo* ('An Invisible Spot in this World'), by renowned film star Juan Diego Botto, premiered in October 2012 (Botto is the son of the disappeared Argentine actor Diego Botto and Cristina Rota, the aforementioned Argentine founder of Madrid's Sala Mirador). The piece consists of five short monologues on migration. One of them (*Locutorio* ('Phone Booth')) features an Argentine economic (illegal) immigrant in a telephone booth, talking to his wife across the ocean about his precarious work situation following the 2008 financial crisis.

Arguably the best example of this phenomenon was *En construcción* ('Under Construction'), the debut play by Argentine playwright and actress Carolina Román, co-authored with Nelson Dante and directed by her partner, the Spanish actor Tristán Ulloa. Born in 2007 as a short piece, six years later (in 2013) the creative team opted to expand it to incorporate issues relating to the impact of the 2008 financial crisis in Spain. The result was a piece on a young Argentine couple trying their luck in Madrid, where the crisis tests and eventually breaks their relationship. The piece was well received in several small fringe venues, taking part, for instance, in the first season of the Teatro del Barrio, a participatory cultural project (it still operates as a cooperative) created in December 2013 under the banner of the anti-austerity Indignados movement.

The appearance of these two productions in the same year was not down to

---

[14] Immigration was one of the central topics exploited by the traditions of the *sainete criollo* and *grotesco criollo*. As Werth (2010: 142) states, they 'represent separate stages in the immigration project: the *sainete criollo* documents the building of community and fosters integration of immigrants while the *grotesco criollo* offers a disillusioned, psychological assessment of the project's outcome'.

chance. Debate around the topic of immigration was fuelled by the approval in April 2012 of the 16/2012 Decree, which restricted undocumented immigrants' access to the Spanish public health system (an issue explicitly mentioned in *Un trozo invisible de este mundo*). With both coming from a Stanislavskian realist Argentine tradition — Botto trained at his mother's school and Román with Raúl Serrano — it is hardly surprising that the two productions adopted an overtly realist, albeit sentimental style (especially in the case of Román's piece, which, nevertheless, alters the chronological order of the breakup story, in the fashion of Pinter's *Betrayal*).

This was also a hallmark of another piece addressing the same topic during this period: Pablo Messiez's *The Eyes* (2011). Premiered before *Un trozo invisible de este mundo* and the long version of *En construcción*, the subject of immigration is addressed from a different stylistic standpoint in this piece. The process of creation and structure must be understood in connection to the abovementioned post-1980s renewal of theatrical languages in Argentina. For Messiez, *The Eyes* was the first piece in which he had the chance to explore freely what would later become his personal directorial language, and this is evident in the way the text, the acting and the space design interact, as the next section will show.

'The Eyes': Love, Migration and Displacement from a Non-Realist Perspective

Re-writing Pérez Galdós's 'Marianela'

The Eyes belongs to the twenty-first-century Argentine alternative theatrical tradition of rewriting canonical texts (see p. 10), radically adapting Pérez Galdós's novel *Marianela* for the problematic present. Published three years before Galdós's *La desheredada* (1881) — the novel usually credited with introducing naturalism to the Spanish context — *Marianela* (1878) is set in the (fictional) mining town of Socartes, in the northern region of Cantabria, an area experiencing a (late) industrial revolution. The narrative begins with the arrival of the ophthalmologist and first-person narrator Teodoro Golfín to the town, on a visit to his brother. In Socartes, Golfín meets Pablo (the blind son of a wealthy landowner) as well as the poor orphan Nela (Pablo's guide and sweetheart). Employing the latest advances in science, Golfín eventually succeeds in curing Pablo's congenital blindness.[15] *Marianela* is heavily infused with positivist philosophy and influenced by Auguste Comte's law of three stages: the principle that the evolution of human societies passes through three stages as regards their understanding of the world (the theological, supernatural

---

[15] For a comparison between Galdós's novel and Messiez's adaptation from a disability studies perspective see Willem (2018).

or religious; the metaphysical or rational; and the positive or empirical). In almost allegorical fashion, the main characters (Marianela, Pablo and Golfín) embody these three stages. Galdós's vision of the results of 'progress' is not, however, unequivocal. Pablo's successful operation, for example, has a negative impact on his perception of Nela. His entrance into the visual world (and its rules of beauty) destroys his idealistic relationship with the poor orphan and provokes her demise (a broken heart is given as the suggested cause for the sudden and mysterious illness that kills her). As Anderson states (2015: 927), '*Marianela* sets up a complex and nuanced system of pluses and minuses, of ambiguous outcomes, and in particular lingers on the pathos of those necessary losses' in a process of modernisation.

In terms of plot, *The Eyes* does not constitute a significant departure from Galdós's text. Nevertheless, and leaving to one side the different parameters of page and stage, it is a different proposition as regards exposition. While *Marianela* depicts the nascent effects of industrialisation in Spain, Messiez offers some hints at the (now global) problems associated with the latest stages of this modernisation process and, in particular, domestic and foreign migration. Set in a small town in contemporary Spain (the exact location is never given), *The Eyes* focuses its attention on the doomed lovers, reducing the plot to four characters: Pablo, Nela, Doctor Chabuca Granda (a female substitute for Galdós's Golfín), and an additional new character, Natalia, Nela's young and beautiful mother. Pablo's guide and sweetheart Nela is no longer a poor orphan but rather an Argentine immigrant living with her mother — the two women had first come to Spain in pursuit of Natalia's Italian lover, Andrea, who has subsequently disappeared from their life. Like Galdós's Golfín, Chabuca Granda arrives as a tourist in Pablo's town, a town affected by the alarming depopulation of rural areas, the phenomenon known as the 'empty' or 'emptied Spain' ('We're all leaving this place. Everybody leaves small towns. Except for the old people, who couldn't get out in time', says Natalia in her last farewell to the public; see p. 53).

Galdós's original opposition between the urban and the rural is further complicated by Natalia and Nela's double migration: they have moved first from Tucumán to Buenos Aires (where the mother studied philosophy) and then to Spain. While Nela longs for her life back in what she considers to be her home, Natalia thinks that 'Tucumán is full of ignorant people' (p. 28) and identifies herself instead with the more 'civilised' culture of Buenos Aires.[16] Nela's mother

---

[16] Although not shown in the piece, this previous migration movement inside Argentina is represented in *The Eyes* through the different accents of mother (from Buenos Aires) and daughter (from Tucumán), but also hinted at in the sporadic references to some of the binary oppositions characteristic of Argentina's own national imaginary, such as Buenos Aires/the *interior* (the term used to refer to the rest of the country that is not the capital city), or civilisation/barbarism. For a discussion of the topic, which suggests abandoning the term *interior*, see DeMaria (2014).

embraces a sense of deterritorialization: 'when you leave a place, it's like you cut off a piece of yourself. [...] You cut it off and it can heal, but you're still left with a scar. People over there are going to tell you you're from here, and here they'll tell you you're from over there. Which is okay in the end. Because you're not from anywhere' (p. 46). Unlike the migrant characters of *En construcción* or *Un trozo invisible de este mundo*, Nela and Natalia have seemingly cut ties with their relatives in Argentina. The figures of Nela's uncle (Walter) and (deceased) grandmother (Nené) are recalled by mother and daughter almost as part of a mythical past, subject to multiple interpretations (for instance, when both characters discuss the wart on Nené's forehead; see p. 45).

To complicate this displaced identity, Natalia is shown also to hold strong ties to her Italian background (Italy is also the homeland of her lover Andrea). For Natalia, in fact, love is the only thing that gives a sense of belonging ('You know where your place is? Where someone loves you' (p. 47)). But love turns out to be equally transitory. If Andrea abandoned Natalia, a similar fate awaits Nela. Natalia's prediction to Pablo ('Nela is not for you. She's ugly and she's poor. [...] I'm very honest. But not stupid. [...] I know you will want someone like you when you're cured' (p. 39)) comes to pass in a manner akin to Galdós's novel. While *The Eyes* might be more tightly focused on amorous as opposed to economic precarity, Argentina's financial woes are referenced on multiple occasions. When Nela confesses that she would like to return to Tucumán, her mother instantly dismisses the idea: 'Everyone's either very poor or very rich. And guess which group we'd be in' (p. 46). (Tucumán, in fact, belongs to one of the regions of Argentina (the north-west) with the highest income inequality rate; see CEPAL 2016: 34.) It is no coincidence that Messiez drew inspiration for the creation of Nela's world — especially her very personal, almost pagan, cult of the Virgin Mary — from Lucrecia Martel's film *La ciénaga*, a work similarly set in Argentina's disadvantaged north-west region.[17]

As in Martel's film, Messiez's play also breaks the hegemonic (future-focused) structure of conventional realist narrative and gives prominence, instead, to the present time of the performance and the audience watching it. To achieve this effect, he uses different strategies. Beyond its indebtedness to Galdós's source novel, allusions and quotations abound in *The Eyes*. To give just one example, Natalia employs lines from Chekhov's *Three Sisters* in her final monologue. The result is a distancing effect that prevents the audience from being completely immersed in the fictional world. Elsewhere, Natalia's rumination on love and smoking (Scene 10) was written, according to Messiez, to challenge Fernanda

---

[17] Nela's religiosity is described in Galdós's *Marianela* as a strange compound of paganism and sentimentality (Pérez Galdós 2001: 160). In a similar popular religious vein, in Lucrecia Martel's film the background sound of the TV, constantly on, brings news about an apparition of the Virgin Mary on the side of a water tank in a nearby town.

Orazi in the role. The intended result was for the audience to experience her speech almost as if it were an aria in an opera, an independent segment where the action is paused, and we delight in the rhythms and music of the words (see Solé 2021), a point to which I will return.

By contrast, the climactic moment of Pablo's cure and its eventual consequences are almost completely suppressed. If Galdós accelerates the end of his novel (after Pablo recovers his sight, Marianela dies from a strange disease in just a few days), in *The Eyes* the even more mysterious death of Nela (perhaps a car accident or by her own hand) and the departure of Pablo are only briefly acknowledged in Natalia's last long monologue to the audience. The textual component was not, however, given prominence within Orazi's performance of this monologue. The same is even more obviously true of the preceding wordless moment in which Pablo, freed from the bandages that cover his eyes, finally sees: the actor's body language and means of engaging with the audience are transformed.

A telluric melodrama

Messiez's work with the actors in *The Eyes* is in important respects heir to the *teatro de estados* tradition and Bartís's ideas about theatre. For instance, the sub-title of *The Eyes* (*A Telluric Melodrama*) must be understood within this framework ('telluric', here means 'folkloric', but it is also related to the way in which the native soil shapes its inhabitants). With its surprising juxtaposition of styles and genres, it brings to mind, for instance, the sub-title of Bartís's *Postales argentinas* (1988): *Sainete de ciencia ficción* ('Argentine Postcards: A Science Fiction Sainete'). Such 'stylistic mixtures' are inextricable linked to what Dubatti (drawing on the playwright Mauricio Kartún) calls *cirujeo cultural* ('cultural scavenging'), which has been a hallmark of Argentine alternative theatre since the renovations of the late eighties.[18] In addition to the aforementioned intertextuality, hybridity is expressed in *The Eyes* through the use of a plurality of acting languages. Melodrama, a genre traditionally dismissed by the Argentine realist tradition, comes, as was often the case in the *teatro de estados*, to the fore. The performances of Nela and, especially, Natalia are designed to exacerbate sorrow and anger with the express aim of turning the stage into 'a space of extremes, of the extra-quotidian' (see p. 63). The aforementioned reflection on smoking and love (Scene 10), the final conversation between Natalia and the phone company (while trying to contact Andrea, in Scene 13),[19] or the subsequent dialogue between mother and daughter, are

---

[18] One of Kartún latest and most successful plays, *Terrenal* ('Earthly'), has a similar compound sub-title: *Pequeño misterio ácrata* ('A Little Libertarian/Anarchist Mystery'), mixing the tradition of the allegorical medieval mystery play with disputes over land and property from the political movement.

all conceived to be acted with a variety of registers ranging from emotional authenticity to the artifice of melodrama.[20] Casting was paramount: both actresses had backgrounds in Argentina's alternative circuit and their virtuoso display of different acting styles was highlighted by numerous Spanish reviews of the production (see, for instance, Ordóñez 2011).

The Eyes similarly crafts the sound of words and the rhythm of dialogues, especially as regards the combination of fast-paced (sometimes even overlapping) lines and moments of silence. This is a popular style of acting in Argentine alternative theatre, used by *teatristas* as different as Bartís, Veronese, Spregelburd and Tolcachir (see Saura-Clares 2021: 11). Such techniques will be immediately obvious to anyone watching the recording of Scene 2 of the original production (see note 4) in which Pablo, Nela and Natalia deliver their speeches.

Messiez's signature style is distinguished by a focus on the actor's work on *repercusión* ('repercussion', but also 'resonance' or 'reverberation') as opposed to action. When, for example, an actor speaks on stage, they need to focus on the effect of their words (sound and meaning) on others, as much as on themselves. As he states in his theatrical notebook for the play *El tiempo que estemos juntos* ('The Time We Would Spend Together'): 'Actuar es saberse en relación. Con el cuerpo abierto a dejarse hacer mientras hace' ('Acting is about knowing that you are connected to the rest of what is happening. With the body open to being affected while also doing', Messiez 2019: 135). *The Eyes*, in this sense, consolidated a line of exploration surrounding music and *repercusión* that Messiez further explored in later work such as his 2019 production of *Las canciones* ('The Songs'). If music is often considered a manipulative device for eliciting emotional responses, Messiez uses it as a tool to create continuity between what is happening on stage and in the stalls. Usually acknowledged by the characters (for instance, when Chabuca listens to Nina Simone in Scene 9, or when Nela dances with Pablo in Scene 7), the audience witnesses how music is affecting (in real time) the bodies of the actors.

Tainted love: Space in 'The Eyes'

Following successful productions by Veronese and Tolcachir, simple living/home settings (so frequent in fringe productions) became stylistic shorthand

---

[19] Here there is another moment of intertextuality, since the acting of Orazi evokes the work of Anna Magnani in Rossellini's film version of Cocteau's *The Human Voice*, in the anthology film *Love* (1948).

[20] This formal exploration of the act of crying, in fact, also recalls *Cachetazo de campo* ('Countryside Slap', 1998), the first work as director by another important former student of Bartís and the Sportivo Teatral, Federico León. The piece — which like *The Eyes* also featured a mother and daughter who have recently moved to the countryside — was an authentic tour de force for the two actresses, who spent most of the show modulating their continuous (and apparently unjustified) bursting into tears.

for Argentine productions among Spanish critics and audiences.[21] With *The Eyes*, Messiez sought for the first time in his then short career as a director to distance himself from this tradition of spatial design. In a tribute to Pina Bausch's setting for her choreographing of Stravinski's *The Rite of Spring* (1975), the almost empty stage was covered in unstable piles of soil, deeply conditioning the movement and look of the actors, who ended up stained with dirt. As Messiez remarks (see p. 61), this served to tell, by means of the theatrical space, of the continuous exile that the characters of Nela and Natalia suffer, their continuous movement from one place to the other also recalling the sacrificial dance of death that closes Stravinsky's piece. This set design was charged with meaning when Natalia packed her suitcase, filling it with soil that she grabbed from the ground. The few objects on stage (a tiny bed and a table) functioned as an almost parodic deconstruction of the living room set, while the artificial and conventional nature of the theatrical space (and of theatre in general) is openly acknowledged several times by the characters. For instance, when Chabuca asks Nela how she entered her B&B room, Nela simply replies 'There's no door here' (p. 36), highlighting the fact that the set did not include any doors or other spatial demarcation. Nela's Virgin Mary statuette with the head of a doll connects with the use of old, sometimes extravagant or broken objects, so treasured by some Argentine practitioners (it is, in fact, another stylistic manifestation of the aforementioned 'cultural scavenging').[22]

Messiez himself sees *The Eyes* as his first step towards an authorial stamp in his writing for/on the stage. This personal signature, nevertheless, was enabled by the opportunities allowed by the Spanish theatrical system and its public funding (in this case, the Fernán Gómez theatre). *The Eyes* can be seen as a 'best of both worlds' coming together of two theatrical traditions that provides us with a gateway for better understanding the transatlantic trajectory of a figure now firmly established as one of the most exciting and invigorating names on the contemporary Spanish (and Hispanic) stage.

---

[21] Privileging the work of actors over an elaborate *mise en scène* was, to an extent, born of necessity, but frequently it was also an aesthetic strategy and choice. Daniel Veronese, for instance, often openly chooses to dispense with music and lighting design and reuses the same setting for different productions (see Villarreal 2019).

[22] The manipulation of old dolls, for instance, reappears in several shows by Periférico de Objetos, such as *El hombre de arena* ('The Sandman'). In addition to generating a feeling sometimes close to the Freudian uncanny, as Ferreyra (2019) has wisely noticed, many times this use of worn-out, old-fashioned objects connects with the aforementioned reflection on Argentina's identity as a failed national project, especially in the work of Bartís (see Cornago 2006).

THE EYES
A TELLURIC MELODRAMA

1. WHAT YOU'RE LISTENING TO IS MY MIND

Complete darkness.

PABLO   Hello. Evening, everyone. No need to worry. There's nothing wrong with the lights. This is… a bit of an experiment. I don't quite know where to begin. My name is Pablo. I was born blind. What you're listening to is my mind. You're seeing what I see. Well, not exactly. That would imply that my mind is like the half-darkness that you're in now. But I don't even know what darkness is. Or what shadows are. From the beginning, I have inhabited a complete void. Nothing has a form — not even in dreams. I dream sounds. My world is a world of textures, voices, smells, tastes. You can't imagine this because you can see. Your minds are full of images, and they have always been there. They will shape even how you imagine their absence. My world, on the other hand, is abstract. Very little is certain. Save a few things. Like how much I enjoy being with Nela. We're in her house now. (*Light on* Natalia *and* Nela's *house*) She brought me here to meet her mother. I insisted. She didn't like the idea at all. But she loves me, and she agreed. So, here we are: my Nela, Natalia and me. And it's not going well.

2. LOOK ME IN THE EYES

Natalia *and* Nela's *house, interior. The lights are on.* Pablo, Nela *and* Natalia *are speaking.* Natalia *is making absurd gestures. She has realised that she can do whatever she wants in front of* Pablo, *and this amuses her.*[1]

NELA   Enough, mum.

NATALIA   Why? He doesn't mind. Do you mind?

PABLO   What?

NATALIA   (*Addressing* Nela) See? He doesn't mind.

PABLO   I couldn't wait to meet you, Ms Genovesi.

NATALIA   Ms Genovesi! God. Such formality in a young man.

---

[1] In the original Spanish-language production, Nela and Natalia speak with two distinct Argentine accents. Nela's accent is from Tucumán, and Natalia's is from the capital city, Buenos Aires.

PABLO   Well… you're Nela's mother. Also, you just called me 'young man'.

NELA   (*Addressing* Pablo) Shall we head off?

PABLO   But we've just arrived.

NATALIA   (*Overlapping, almost at the same time*) But you've only just arrived. (*Addressing* Pablo) So? What have you heard about me? (*Addressing* Nela) Hey, what have you told him?

NELA   Can you get us a drink, we're thirsty.

NATALIA   Get it yourself. This is your house too.

NELA   Wine?

PABLO   Wine would be perfect.

NELA   Right.

Nela *leaves — she will return in a few moments with a bottle of wine and wine glasses. Meanwhile,* Natalia *describes* Nela's *movements to* Pablo.

NATALIA   Nela's walking to the kitchen. Nela, bring the wine glasses! Right now, she's getting the glasses, oh, now she's coming in with the wine. And now we're going to the living room.

NELA   He's not deaf, mum.

NATALIA   I'm just trying to make him feel included.

Nela *carefully attends to all of* Pablo's *needs. She pushes the wine glass closer to him, trying to make him appear self-sufficient, to make his blindness less obvious. They all have their glasses now.*

NATALIA   Well, cheers to us.

PABLO   To you both.

NATALIA   If you say so. You can relax, young man. (*Clinking glasses with* Nela) In the eyes, love, you have to look each other in the eyes. Or you *know* what will happen.[2] (Nela *gestures towards* Pablo) Well, he has eyes, doesn't he?

PABLO   (*Overlapping, almost at the same time*) Yes, in the eyes, Nelly. Look me in the eyes.

NATALIA   (*Amused*) Ah…. This is quite something. You're a good match.

---

[2] The myth goes that toasting without making eye contact brings bad luck (and seven years of bad sex).

Awkward pause. Natalia *is still fascinated by the fact that a blind man is in her house.*

NELA   Well, we really should be off. We've got to go, mum.

PABLO   So soon?

NATALIA   (*Overlapping*) You go. Leave us adults alone.

NELA   We're all adults here.[3]

NATALIA   Go. Go and make some maté! Has he tried maté?[4]

NELA   What about the wine?

NATALIA   (*Emptying her glass over the floor*)[5] There's no more wine.

PABLO   (*Addressing them both*) Please don't worry about it. It's fine. I'm very happy with wine.

NATALIA   Come on! Are you sure you don't want to try maté?

PABLO   We could try it later if Nela's not up for it.

NATALIA   (*Addressing* Nela) Would it bother you tremendously to go make the maté now?

NELA   No.

NATALIA   Then go!

NELA   I'll be right back.

Nela *leaves.*

NATALIA   Communication is key.

PABLO   Yes.

Pause.

---

[3] This metatheatrical comment plays with the fact that in the original production all the actors were about the same age.
[4] Maté is a traditional South American infused drink made with dried leaves of *yerba mate*. The leaves are served in a container with a metal straw, into which hot water is periodically poured.
[5] In the original production the stage was covered with soil. In the Spanish text the word *tierra* (translated in this version alternately as 'land', 'dirt' or 'soil') has different denotative and connotative associations. It points to the context (the play is set in a small town in the Spanish countryside), but also to the sense of belonging and the feeling of uprootedness of those who leave their country of origin.

NATALIA   (*Looking at him very closely*) You know, I've always been terrified of going blind. I've always thought it was the worst thing that could happen to someone. I am from Tucumán and the nights there can get so dark. When I was a child, I would always leave a light on at night. I was terrified of going blind without realising it.

PABLO   I was born this way. So it's all I know.

NATALIA   Yes, of course. If it's all you know then… it's all you know.

Pause.

NATALIA   So. You like Nela?

PABLO   She's a beautiful person.

NATALIA   Well, she's very sweet. (*Pause*) Not beautiful. Not quite. Not at all. You know that, right?

PABLO   Well, I like her.

NATALIA   No, of course, if you like her, then that's… I'm just letting you know. You're good-looking and I think you should know the truth. Yes, you're blind and it won't be easy for you to find someone patient enough to deal with your… issue. I'll admit that Nelly is very patient. Patience is definitely one of her virtues. But when it comes to her face or her body… I'm going to be completely frank with you. I may be her mother, but I'm not in denial and I know that we're stuck.

PABLO   I know what her face and body are like. What do you mean, *stuck*?

NATALIA   Stuck in the shit. How do you know what they are like?

PABLO   I've touched them.

NATALIA   Oh, yes, that thing you do… right. That's not the same though. Well, who knows really… I don't know anything about blind people. I don't feel sorry for you, for what it's worth. Do you see what I mean? I'm very straightforward. At my age one gets straight to the point. And the point is, I don't feel sorry for you.

PABLO   I'm glad.

NATALIA   As you should be. Pity is a very ugly thing. Let me tell you a story. This happened on a bus once, in Buenos Aires. I was on the bus and two blind men suddenly got on. Naturally they sat at the front, in the disabled area. A few minutes later, at another stop, another blind person got on. A very big blind woman. The whole thing was odd already, because blind people tend to be thin, like you.

PABLO   Not really. There are all sorts.

NATALIA   Anyway, this fat woman, fat and blind, after paying for her ticket waltzes off directly towards the disabled seats. The two blind men shout out that the seats are occupied. So really offended, she screams back: I'M BLIND and they respond WE'RE BLIND, TOO. (*Laughs*) The woman completely froze. And then the bus driver got involved and asked for someone to 'please give the blind woman a seat'. No, sorry, the 'visually impaired' woman, those were his words. What an idiot. *Visually impaired*. I hate euphemisms. They put me on edge. What would you call yourself? Blind? Or visually impaired?

PABLO   I'd say blind. I actually like to be called blind.

NATALIA   Blind. Well, love is blind too…[6]

PABLO   Where's Nela?

NATALIA   She's making maté. What's wrong? Am I making you uncomfortable?

PABLO   No. Not at all.

NATALIA   Let's try something. Touch me. Touch my face and tell me what I look like.

PABLO   Now?

NATALIA   Yes, now. Didn't you say that you see things by touching them? If you weren't blind, you'd already know what I look like, right? So it's fine, right? (*Pause*) Do you want me to call Nela? NELA!

Nela *enters without the maté.*

NATALIA   Come here. Your boyfriend is going to look at my face.

Pablo *approaches* Natalia. *He begins to touch her face.*

PABLO   Nela, I'm going to touch your mother's face. (*He does*) Your skin is very soft.

NATALIA   Soft, he says, soft.

PABLO   Very youthful.

NATALIA   (*Alluding to* Nela) Yes, I had her very young.

NELA   Listen, mum, we need to go. We're leaving.

---

[6] In the original Spanish text, Natalia's response is a pun. She says 'sos ciego' ('you're blind') and then suddenly realizes that in her Argentine Spanish this sounds exactly the same as the word *sosiego* ('tranquility' or 'quietude'), celebrating the phonetic coincidence. While in many regions of Spain the letter 'c' followed by 'i' is pronounced as the English 'th' (/θ/) in *theatre*, in Argentina it sounds like an 's' (/s/) as in *sad*.

PABLO   What about the maté?

NELA   It didn't come out right. It's burnt. Come on.[7]

PABLO   Goodbye, Natalia. Thank you for everything.

Nela *takes* Pablo's *hand and drags him away.* Natalia *remains. Now alone, she touches her face.*

NATALIA   See you soon.

3. SUCH SMALL HANDS

Pablo *and* Nela *are in a field.*

PABLO   Your mother is quite something.

NELA   Yeah. Quite something. Quite in-your-face. Let's sit here.

PABLO   She's beautiful.

NELA   Yeah. I heard you the first time. Enough about my mother. Tell me about yours. What was she like?

PABLO   I don't know. She died when she saw I was blind.

NELA   Jesus. I'm so sorry... And... your dad? Did you know him?

PABLO   Yeah. He was a good man. He taught me everything I know. He used to sing to me. And read me poems.

NELA   He read you poems! That's never happened to me, ever. Recite one, please. Nobody has ever done that for me. Recite one that you remember.

PABLO   Okay, this is my favourite one. I'm going to say it with my eyes closed. A little gift for my Nela.

> somewhere i have never travelled, gladly beyond
> any experience, your eyes have their silence:
> in your most frail gesture are things which enclose me,
> or which i cannot touch because they are too near
>
> your slightest look easily will unclose me
> though i have closed myself as fingers,
> you open always petal by petal myself as Spring opens
> (touching skilfully, mysteriously) her first rose

---

[7] Maté is made with water at approximately 80° C. Nela says that the maté 'didn't come out right' and it's undrinkable because the water has boiled over and burnt the plant leaves used to make the beverage.

or if your wish be to close me, i and
my life will shut very beautifully, suddenly,
as when the heart of this flower imagines
the snow carefully everywhere descending;

nothing which we are to perceive in this world equals
the power of your intense fragility: whose texture
compels me with the colour of its countries,
rendering death and forever with each breathing

(i do not know what it is about you that closes
and opens; only something in me understands
the voice of your eyes is deeper than all roses)
nobody, not even the rain, has such small hands[8]

Pause.

PABLO   Are you okay?

NELA   I… I don't know what to say. (*Pause*) The sky is so beautiful right now.

PABLO   What is it like?

NELA   Enormous and pink. Sometimes at night, when I can't sleep, I try and find a spot in the sky to look at. I look for a small cluster of stars, and for a second, I feel like I'm back in Tucumán. But there were loads more stars there. So here I just look for a couple of stars and imagine all the rest. Mum says that there weren't actually more stars in Tucumán. Just less light. Do you believe in God?

PABLO   Yes.

NELA   Mmm. I do too, a bit. But I have more faith in my Virgin Mary. You know, I speak to her. I talk to her about you.

PABLO   About me? What do you say?

NELA   (*Pause*) That's private.

PABLO   And does she respond?

NELA   How on Earth should she respond! Hey — I'm not stupid. She's a statue.

PABLO   I didn't say you were stupid. I'm just kidding. How could I say something like that? You're my darling. And very wise.

NELA   Since you like my mother so much, you should know that she thinks religion is a joke. She might be beautiful, but she's a complete atheist. Talking

---

[8] This poem is from E. E. Cummings's poetry collection *ViVa* (1931).

to Mary is good for me. I hear myself as I speak to her, and things suddenly become clear.

PABLO   Why did you leave Tucumán?

NELA   Oh... For a lot of reasons. Mostly because mum wanted to study in Buenos Aires. According to her, Tucumán is full of ignorant people. She said that if we stayed, she'd end up hanging herself on an aguaribay.

PABLO   On a what?

NELA   It's a type of big tree from there. She found a way to study philosophy in Buenos Aires thanks to her uncle Walter, who was gay and really well-educated. You wanna know something? I realised later that every Walter in Tucumán was gay. But that's not something we talked about much. I did make a note of it, though. All the Walters were gentle, and they wore perfume.

PABLO   So then you set off for Buenos Aires?

NELA   Yeah, exactly. We didn't take a thing with us, either. We even left Granny. Alone, with the dog. Anyway, all along mum had been saying that she was drowning in Tucumán but studying made it worse. She kept getting more and more sad. All she did was read and smoke. Read and smoke. I could see there was something rotten inside of her. But everything changed when she met Andrea. Who was a man, by the way. In Italy apparently you can have a girl's name and be a man. And he was Italian.

PABLO   Did she meet him at the University?

NELA   No. Well, actually, yes, but he wasn't a student there. He came to a very important book launch. People came from all around to listen. Even my uncle Walter came. You can't imagine how Buenos Aires had changed him. His eyes were all sparkly.

Pause.

I think in Tucumán, he was a fish out of water. Some people struggle in places like that.

PABLO   Places like what?

NELA   Small places.[9] I mean anywhere that isn't Buenos Aires.

PABLO   I see.

NELA   Anyway, so after the book launch there was a drinks reception, and Andrea was there serving the wine. That's how they met. Mum fell head over

---

[9] In the original Spanish text, Nela uses the word *interior*, the term used in Argentina to refer to the rest of the country that is not the capital city (see note 16, p. 15).

heels for him… He didn't, or at least not as much. She seemed to get worse the more she saw him, but she kept telling me he was the love of her life. I don't know, sometimes I think mum doesn't know what's good for her, she gets all confused… Andrea always sent her flowers and that was nice, it's true. But then mum stopped paying any attention to studying and began to live just for him. And then suddenly he got offered a job here and left. That's when mum sold the house that we had in Tucumán, she gave uncle Walter our dog and we sped off after Andrea. But he never showed up again. And I don't think he's ever going to show up, but mum is still stuck, she's still obsessed, waiting for him. She can say what she likes about being an atheist, but she has a whole lot of faith in Andrea. She may be an atheist, but trust me, she believes. She's even kept the flowers he gave her. She keeps them pressed between some books that she brought over.

PABLO   Poor thing. Love is so complicated.

NELA   Complicated, yes… My mum is complicated.

PABLO   And your dad?

NELA   I don't know, I never met him. She had me at fifteen. It happened a long time ago and she doesn't talk about him. All I know is that he was really short.

PABLO   Just like you. Are you happy you came here?

NELA   Yes. Sometimes.

PABLO   When?

NELA   When we talk to each other… and when I eat toast with olive oil.[10] And when I walk down the streets that I like. And…

Pablo *kisses her passionately.* Nela *wriggles and tries to get away.*

NELA   Oh! Pablo. I'm so sorry, but I have to go. I have to go and do something very important.

Nela *runs off, almost exploding with joy.*

4. I AM IN LOVE

Nela *is with her little statue of the Virgin Mary. It's a plaster statuette. The original head is missing. It has been replaced with the head of one of* Nela's *dolls.*

NELA   (*Addressing the statuette*) Thank you, Blessed Mother! My sweet Virgin Mary! HE KISSED ME! HE KISSED ME! It's so nice to be kissed. Have you ever been kissed? Look. (*She kisses the statuette*) Can you see how nice it feels?

---

[10] Toasted bread with olive oil is a typical breakfast dish in Spain, especially in the south.

You'd like him, Mary. He is a big believer. Seeing may be believing, but I am telling you, Mary, he's never seen a thing, and yet he believes in it all. Can you imagine. He believes in me. In everything that I say. Well, I'm meant to tell him what I see, and I do, but sometimes I don't say everything. I never lie to him, but uhm, you know I take care of him. That's okay, right, Mary? It's not a bad thing, right? That's being caring, right? It's being loving. And he believes me. He loves me, and that is a way of believing, right? He told me I was wise! Me, wise, when all I do is tell him what I see! When I just describe what I see and that's it. But I know he's happy when he's with me. I can tell. And I am happy with him. Even happier when I see him happy. I've never loved anyone before… but now I think I'm in love. I mean I think I am, because this feeling is new and different from anything that came before. My days are now split in two: when I'm with Pablo — that's the best part of the day — and when I'm not with Pablo. When I'm not with him I keep my eyes closed so we feel closer when we're next together. I want to marry him and have babies with him and make them really happy. You know something, Mary? I've realised that I'm happiest when I make the people I love happy. But this makes me feel like I'm being selfish, because in the end what motivates me is just my own happiness. But maybe that's okay? It's okay if we're all happy in the end, right? (*Pause*) Mary, I need to tell you something. I wouldn't mind if the babies were blind. I think I'd actually be a better mum to them if they were. Really. If every year a certain number of blind babies have to be born, I'd gladly do my part and take a share of them. Another mum would mind, but not me. I'd feel better if they couldn't see. Because I know what blind people need. And I want to be there to give them all that. Please, please, I'm begging you to make sure that everything keeps going in the way that it is, and that we get married, and live together, and that we have lots of babies. In exchange, I'll take all the blind babies that you want to send me. Please, Mary. You know I never ask you for anything, but I need you now. I'm asking you to give me Pablo forever. Please. Please. Please. Please. Please. I have to go now. I love you so much. Bye bye.

5. I'M NOT WAITING FOR YOU ANYMORE

While this scene takes place, Nela *sneaks into the house. She puts on some lipstick and an accessory in the shape of a flower that she steals from her mother's purse.*

NATALIA   (*Calling* Andrea *by phone*) It's me. If you hang up, I'll kill you. No, I'm being completely serious. I'll send over some Russians to beat you up and slam you against a wall. (*Pause*) I'm not going to wait for you anymore. You don't make love suffer. Do you understand, you bastard? That's not how it works. Not in my world. And you got in my way. So you better prepare yourself. You've got it coming. You will cry rivers of pain. And you won't be able to make anyone suffer anymore. Not even yourself. Because I'll have sucked out every single ounce of suffering that you could ever experience. You'll become a plant.

A vegetable. A nice little vegetable, you piece of shit. A nice little veg. No! I'm not done! You're dying already, can't you tell. You're dying. We're all dying, but I'm making that extra clear for you because you're such an idiot that you don't even realise it. You're dying and you wasted so much time thinking about what others thought of you, it's such a shame. You ought to be ashamed. What a shame. (*She hangs up. She pours herself a glass of whisky*) Right. That felt good.

6. YOU WERE IN MY DREAM

Pablo *is alone in the field, still waiting for* Nela. *A woman,* Chabuca, *arrives in a hurry. She's wearing joggers, but still looks elegant. She carries a suitcase. It is obvious that she is not from the town. She stops and says:*

CHABUCA   You were in my dream.

PABLO   What? Are you talking to me?

CHABUCA   Yes. You were blind.

PABLO   I am blind. Who are you?

CHABUCA   I know. You were handsome, too.

PABLO   I'm not.

CHABUCA   You don't know that.

PABLO   Who are you?

CHABUCA   This is all very strange, but it's happening all the same.

PABLO   What's happening?

CHABUCA   Finding each other. You have been blind since birth, right?

PABLO   How did you know?

CHABUCA   Because of the dream.

PABLO   Who are you?

CHABUCA   My name is Dr Chabuca Granda.[11]

PABLO   Chabuca Granda is dead. And she was Peruvian.

CHABUCA   I'm a different Chabuca Granda. My parents were big fans of hers.

PABLO   Listen, I'm here with my girlfriend. She went off for a moment, but she's coming back. I don't…

CHABUCA   There is nobody here. I can treat you.

---

[11] Chabuca Granda (1920–1983) was a Peruvian singer and composer.

PABLO   What?

CHABUCA   I am an ophthalmologist. I can cure you.

PABLO   Are you mocking me?

CHABUCA   No. This is unbelievable, but it's happening all the same.

PABLO   Forgive me, but I don't know you.

CHABUCA   These things happen.

PABLO   You haven't even had a look at my eyes.

CHABUCA   I have been looking at you for some time now.

PABLO   There is no cure for what I have.

CHABUCA   Who told you that?

PABLO   My father. That's what they told him. The specialists.

CHABUCA   That must have been a long time ago. May I speak with your father?

PABLO   He's dead.

CHABUCA   God, I'm sorry. (*Pause*) May I ask you one last question. How long has it been since you've had your eyes checked?

PABLO   I can't remember. Ages ago. But what I have is impossible to cure. They made that very clear.

CHABUCA   There's a cure now. Wouldn't you like to be able to see?

PABLO   Of course I'd like to be able to see. Just like you'd like to be able to fly. But hey, you're not a bird. And I am blind. (*Shouting*) NELA!

CHABUCA   Because you want to be.

PABLO   What?

CHABUCA   What is your name?

PABLO   Pablo.

CHABUCA   Look, Pablo, you've got nothing to lose. You can't see a thing now. It can't get any worse. I'm staying in the B&B in town. Why don't you come by tomorrow? I can check your eyes properly, give you a few more details so you can decide. The operation would be a long one, but it will work. Come with your girlfriend if you'd like.

PABLO   She must be around here somewhere. Can you see a short girl with hair like straw?

CHABUCA   I've told you already, we're alone. Alone with the land.¹² Do you want to know something? This land is all I have now. This land and your eyes. If you allow it, your eyes could be the joy of my life. Because that's what it's all about in the end, isn't it? I don't know about you, but I have no idea how to live. What is it about? What is all this? What is all this? I became an ophthalmologist so that I could learn something concrete. And I still have no clue what all this is about. To be honest, the only clues I can find are in songs. Songs taught me that the only thing that matters is finding someone that understands you. That's the joy I was talking about. It's a violent joy. It makes you want to scream like crazy because nothing really matters anymore. Someone understands you, and your world is entirely complete. Just like an apple is complete, beautiful and red. Or green. But complete.

PABLO   Look, I can't stay here with you. I'm worried about Nela. I have to go.

CHABUCA   Oh, of course. I'm sorry. I didn't notice... Sorry, sometimes I start speaking and I can't stop. I spend a lot of time on my own and then this happens. I don't even realise it, I see someone and the floodgates open, and all the water comes rushing out. The words, I mean... It's a metaphor, you see...

PABLO   It's fine... are you sure you got a good look at me? Please look at me. Look at my eyes. (Chabuca *looks at his eyes*) Do you really believe I could see one day?

CHABUCA   I don't believe, I know.

PABLO   Really? Do you really think I will be able to see?

CHABUCA   Yes, Pablo.

PABLO   It's been a long time since I've had them checked, it's true. The last time was when my father was still alive... Tomorrow I'll come by the B&B, at four.

CHABUCA   It's a deal.

PABLO   I'll come with Nela. She's not blind.

CHABUCA   Very well. Wait, take this. Give it to Nela and have her read it to you. (*She takes out a newspaper clip from her bag and gives it to him*)

PABLO   What is it?

CHABUCA   You'll see soon enough.

Chabuca *heads towards her B&B. At the reception desk, she says:*

CHABUCA   Hello. I have a booking under Chabuca Granda.

---

¹² See note 5, p. 23.

7. COME CLOSER TO PERU

Mercedes Sosa's version of the song 'Acércate, cholito' ('Come Closer, Cholito')[13] *can be heard in the distance.*

NELA   Pablo! Pablo! Pablo! I'm back! Listen to this song! I love this song! It's the one I've been telling you about! They're playing it in the fair!

Pablo *asks* Nela *to explain herself. He is upset by her long absence, and also shaken up from the encounter with* Chabuca. Nela *tries to soothe him: she tells him, for example, that she got all dressed up for him. She asks him to smell the lipstick she's wearing and to feel the flower she has put on her hair. Finally,* Pablo *gives in and ends up dancing with his girlfriend. This scene and dance is to be improvised every time and it should last as long as the song 'Acércate, cholito'.*

8. WHAT DO YOU SEE?

PABLO   What do you see?

NELA   Lots of people.

PABLO   What else?

NELA   Tall buildings.

PABLO   What else?

NELA   Cars, motorcycles, people.

PABLO   What else?

NELA   Stores, with nice things in the windows. A dog. A stray dog. A chubby little girl holding her mother's hand. An airplane. A group of men standing in a circle, crying. A queue of people going to a wedding, all very badly dressed, but trying hard. Two nuns carrying grocery bags. A very fat boy, reading. A lady with her mouth open, counting coins. She has really big gums and small teeth, like a rat. A girl crying and smoking at the same time sitting on a bench in the square. A boy with a bouquet of flowers half hidden in his coat. A lost boy dressed like an adult. He must be from the wedding group…

PABLO   (*Interrupting her*) Nelly.

NELA   What?

PABLO   Something strange happened to me and I don't know what to think, but if I don't tell you, I'll feel like I'm hiding something and I don't like to hide anything from you.

---

[13] The term *cholito* means 'young *cholo*'. *Cholo* is used in Spanish to refer to people of mixed heritage (mainly for the mixture of white and indigenous backgrounds).

NELA   What happened? Don't scare me.

PABLO   No, don't be scared. It's nothing bad. It's just that when you left, a woman came up to me, an eye doctor. She says she can cure me.

NELA   What woman? That's not possible… What woman? When did she speak to you?

PABLO   When you left. She says that what I have can be cured now.

NELA   How do you know that she's not crazy, or a liar…? Did she say who she was? We can find out…

PABLO   Chabuca Granda.

NELA   What?

PABLO   Her name is Chabuca Granda. Just like the singer from Peru.

NELA   She's tricked you! How could her name be Chabuca Granda? Love, don't you realise? People see that you're blind and they make fun of you.

PABLO   No! That's her name. I know when I'm being lied to. That woman made me remember that I haven't had anyone check my eyes since my father passed away. Do you realise how long it's been? Science is moving forward, Nela… (*He remembers the clip and hands it to her*) Look.

NELA   What is this?

PABLO   She said you could read it to me. (Nela *reads*) What does it say? (Nela *continues to read*) What does it say?

NELA   Fine, her name is Chabuca Granda! And she's an ophthalmologist, and she's received some award.

PABLO   See! She has an award! What's wrong? Why are you upset?

NELA   I don't want you to get hurt.

PABLO   Nelly, I can assure you that this woman wants to help me. I can feel it. Listen, we've agreed to meet tomorrow and…

NELA   (*Interrupting him*) Oh! So you've agreed to meet already?

PABLO   I told her we would both go.

NELA   You've set it up already! (*She rubs off her lipstick with her hand*) If you've already made up your mind, then why are you even asking me what I think? If you've set up an appointment, just go, there's nothing more to say!

PABLO   Why are you being like this? I don't understand.

NELA   Neither do I. I want to be alone. Leave me alone. (*She runs away*)

PABLO   Nela.

NELA   Leave me alone!

9. EYES ARE EYES.

Chabuca is alone in her room in the B&B.

CHABUCA   Cheese. I'm going to buy some cheese.

The Nina Simone song 'He Needs Me' is playing in the B&B. Chabuca *listens as though the lyrics were talking to her.*

CHABUCA   Oh, what a voice. I love this woman.

Nela *barges in.*

NELA   Are you the eye doctor?

CHABUCA   You frightened me.

NELA   Sorry. Are you the ophthalmologist?

CHABUCA   Yes. How did you get in?

NELA   There's no door here.[14]

CHABUCA   Are you Nela?

NELA   Yes. And I have two questions for you, Doctor.

CHABUCA   Go ahead.

NELA   Is Chabuca Granda your real name?

CHABUCA   Yes. They named me after the singer, and…

NELA   Do you think Pablo will be able to see?

CHABUCA   Yes, Nela.

NELA   Why are you here?

CHABUCA   It's a long story. I wasn't happy at home and…

NELA   And you're happy here?

CHABUCA   I'm getting there.

NELA   Great. Then keep on walking. Maybe you'll finally 'get there' somewhere else.

---

[14] Nela's remark is another example of Messiez's use of metatheatrical comments. There is no door because the production literally employs an empty set.

CHABUCA   I'm sorry?

NELA   We don't want you here.

CHABUCA   I don't understand. Wouldn't it make you happy if your boyfriend could see you? Wouldn't it make you happy to see him happy?

NELA   My boyfriend is happy now. And so am I. We're both happy. We love each other. Do you know how difficult that is? Do you have any idea how difficult it is to find someone in the world who really loves you?

CHABUCA   Yes, I do.

NELA   No, you don't! If you knew, then you would never come here and mess everything up.

CHABUCA   But all I want to do is help. What makes you think that he won't love you if he sees you? If he doesn't, then he didn't love you in the first place.

NELA   Look, *Doctor*, you may have a PhD or whatever, but I don't think you are the right person to give any lessons about love, judging from that miserable look on your face. I know that when Pablo gets his sight back, he will want a tall, rich Spanish woman just like him. I know that and actually you know that too, deep down. My mother knows it. The entire town knows it. It's obvious. He's with me now because he needs me and that is also a kind of love. That is also love. Maybe I haven't read as many books as you have, but there are things I do know. Seeing will confuse him. It will make him think he doesn't love me. He will think that he doesn't love me, can't you see. (*She falls to the ground, crying*) Please, Doctor Chabuca. Please go. Find another blind person. An unhappy one. One that really needs you. Go back to the city and leave us in the town alone. What do you care if it's one blind person or another. Eyes are eyes, after all.

CHABUCA   Pablo seemed happy about this.

NELA   What do you know about Pablo? You don't know anything. Anything at all. I know he likes sweets, I know he likes a poem that he read me, a poem about small hands; I know he likes watermelon and I know he likes me. I know he's happy. Much happier than you are. So stop being selfish and leave us alone. Go away.

Nela *begins to throw handfuls of soil at Chabuca.*[15]

---

[15] See note 5, p. 23.

10. NATALIA SMOKES

Inside Natalia *and* Nela's *house.*

PABLO Is Nela here?

NATALIA No.

PABLO She's not? We were together just now. We had an argument.

NATALIA Already arguing… You two make me laugh. Come here. Have a seat.

PABLO I can't. I need to talk to Nela.

NATALIA She'll be here soon enough. She lives here, doesn't she? Now relax, sit down, let's have a moment to ourselves. I'm going to have a ciggie.[16]

PABLO A what?

NATALIA A cigarette. First, what I do is I grab the cigarette. Then the lighter. I'm lighting the cigarette now. Can you hear?

PABLO Yes. You don't need to describe every movement.

NATALIA Smoking does me good. It used to bother me, the smoke. Not the smoke I swallow, the smoke in the air. But I got used to it. And now I like it. It helps me. Look at me smoking. Can you tell how well I smoke? Now I'm smoking, swallowing all the smoke. I look good doing it. It does me good. For some people, the answer is jogging, or eating fruit. For me, it's smoking. I fill my lungs up to the brim. I was drawn in by the packs that say 'SMOKING KILLS'. It's the best publicity in the end. I have a theory. If killing yourself were easier, then everyone would do it. Imagine there was a pill on sale over the counter. Let's call it 'Enough'… I'm sure it would sell out, and everyone would kill themselves. But then, at the very last moment, I think they'd all regret it. Killing yourself is very difficult. It's even more difficult than living. That's why we save ourselves the regret. Well, that's what I think. Who knows.

Pause.

PABLO Today has been an odd day. But I think it will get better. The weather, I mean.

NATALIA I think everything you've been taught was wrong. And that's the reason why your life is full of misunderstandings. But you know, you're not the only one. We're all in the shit. Me, too: myself included, of course. Me, *inclusive*. When I was at university they taught me this word 'inclusive' and I thought it sounded all wrong. But it's correct. If someone said it though, I thought they

---

[16] The original word in Spanish is *pucho*, the Argentine slang (*lunfardo*) term for cigarettes. Pablo, who is from Spain, doesn't understand the word.

were trying to say 'included' and had got it wrong. And why? Why did I see it as a mistake? Because I didn't know the word 'inclusive'. Even though the word existed. It exists. I only knew 'included', so 'inclusive' sounded wrong. The same applies to cigarettes. People know the cons of smoking. They're there on the pack on full display. But what nobody talks about are the pros. Those are taboo, guilty pleasures. Non-smokers live their lives looking down at you. They're just like those rich people that donate money to charities, or that 'rent out', sorry *adopt*, children from strange countries just to give them weird names like Equinox or something similarly absurd. They walk the 'path of virtue'. Well that's what they *think*, because that's what they were taught. They don't know the other path. And since they don't know it, they say it's bad. I've spent a long time thinking about this misunderstanding. It's very sad. I didn't talk to anybody about it, not even Nela. But I'm telling you because you're blind. Which means that for the rest of the world, you're someone to be pitied. And pity is a very bad thing. It's like a big old muffler. It will stop anyone from listening to you. That's why I can talk to you, because of the misunderstanding I mentioned. The only person who will take you seriously, who will really see you, is another blind person. The rest don't understand blindness, it doesn't exist for them, and that's why they think it's a bad thing. That's why the most they can do is pity you. Or take advantage of you. Like I'm doing now, talking to you as though I were talking to myself. Please forgive me, Pablo. I didn't mean to bother you. Listen, I'm going to tell you something useful. Nela is not for you. She's ugly and she's poor. At the end of the day, you're going to want someone like yourself. I'm going to be perfectly frank with you. I told you already: I'm very honest. But not stupid. I'm not stupid. I know you will want someone like you when you're cured. Which is fine. There's nothing wrong with that. Like attracts like. And it makes sense. Life is so incomprehensible, sometimes you just want to crawl in a hole and die, so of course you look for others like yourself. Oh, and that line 'what is essential is invisible to the eyes' is a terrible lie that works when you're a teenager and you believe in essences and life after death and all that. Then you get older, and all you care about is skin. Skin is all that matters. The skin that you see. I'm not talking about touch. I'm not a hippie. I'm talking about sight. You'll see. Eyes are very important, darling. They give you all the clues. I'm not saying that what you see is always what you get, but it's the tip of the iceberg. And you won't ever see what's beneath the tip. Nor will you want to. Because if you see it, that means you're dead. Are you following me? Stone cold and frozen dead. So be happy with what you can see, eat it up. Smoke a lot, and take advantage of your tip of the iceberg, because you have death and eternity to explore what's underneath. If you think what I'm saying is pessimistic or dark, you're an idiot. And it would be a shame, because I think I'm saying things that are worth listening to. This is coming from deep inside me, from the need to understand this madness. And the only thing that gives it any meaning is happiness. I find it soothing that the other side is just for the dead. And *i morti non parlano*,[17] so it doesn't exist for us. It's not that I'm jumping with joy. I just try to be happy, and sometimes it works. A bastard once made me very unhappy, and now what makes me unhappy is not being able to remove his memory like you remove a tumour. I can get used to it during the day, but not at night. At night I have nightmares where he appears to remind me that I chose to drown myself in a dark well with him. Here's another misunderstanding for you. Love. No, worse: passion. Darling, don't trust anyone who talks about passion. Passion has a very good reputation. Just like not smoking, eating vegetables and adopting children from faraway lands. So then you let yourself get hurt because you think that's what passionate love is. You'll lose yourself, because you think that's what love is.

Pause.

PABLO   Are you alright, Natalia?

NATALIA   You are such a darling. On my way here, following the bastard, I went through the airport in Buenos Aires and I didn't have anything to read. All I had were a few of Nela's children's books. And I was sad, and I needed something to distract me. That was when I remembered a book that I had read at university. A book about love, by Barthes. Did they ever read Barthes to you? No? What a shame. Anyway. He was a French poof that wrote beautiful things. That book is beautiful. So I went to the airport bookstore, one of those where they sell best-sellers, and magazines about people that adopt children, and self-help books, and all that Yankee shit with gilded titles. Since I was sad (and when I am very sad or very happy I lose track of where I am and what's going on, I go a little crazy), since I was sad I asked: 'Do you have *A Lover's Discourse: Fragments*?' in the *airport*, in Ezeiza, can you imagine?[18] An absurd request. But, believe it or not, they did have it. I took it as a sign (I was all into essences and romanticism then). I bought it, read it, and justified my entire masochistic journey to Europe from that one book. Of course, it wasn't the book's fault. The book is beautiful. It's more beautiful than smoking, even. But I read it at the wrong time. I was in love. It's not a book to be read when you're in love, because we're all idiots when we're in love. It's meant to be read in the in-between periods, so you can fall in love better the next time. But I read it at the wrong time and it made me think suffering was good. That said, you can learn from suffering. Do you know what I learned? (*Pause*) That suffering is not good. That love is in the tip of the iceberg, in the skin that you see. And it's beautiful. It's that someone takes care of you and loves you, because you take care of and love them. And it's truth. Love is true. I don't trust anything else. Anything about how bad smoking is, or how good milk is. Let someone come to me and tell me

---

[17] 'The dead don't speak' in Italian.
[18] Ezeiza is the main international airport in Buenos Aires.

they're not killing themselves in some way or another. To live is to kill oneself. Living is dying, little by little, there is no other way. You just have to pick the form. That's what's important. To die beautifully. And I am very beautiful when I smoke.

Pause.

PABLO   Natalia, I should go and look for Nela.

NATALIA   (*Pouring some wine into a glass*) Would you like something to drink, Pablo? Look, look, I've served you something already, it's already there.

PABLO   I'm worried. I'd rather go.

NATALIA   Then go, Pablo. Go.

11. DON'T HURT ME

Chabuca *is at the station, waiting for a train.* Pablo *arrives and stumbles over her suitcase.*

PABLO   Oh… I am sorry, madam… (Chabuca *tries to pretend she's someone else. She doesn't do a very good job.*) Chabuca? Is that you?

CHABUCA   Pablo! Yes, of course. What a coincidence! I was just about to give you a call, but since this place is so… rural, I didn't know…

PABLO   Know what?

CHABUCA   How to contact you and… anyway. How lucky that I've found you.

PABLO   What a coincidence!

CHABUCA   Indeed. What are you doing here?

PABLO   I'm looking for Nela.

CHABUCA   Oh.

PABLO   You haven't seen her?

CHABUCA   Me? No, no.

PABLO   Of course, how silly of me, you haven't even met her. I don't know what I'm saying anymore.

CHABUCA   That's right, we've never met, so… I wouldn't recognise her. Perhaps I have seen her and I didn't realise.

PABLO   Anyway, you said you were looking for me. Why?

CHABUCA   I was, yes… An issue has come up and I need to return to the city urgently.

PABLO   Why?

CHABUCA   Well... A call came in and I need to return to the city. An urgent issue. At work. These things happen, you know.

PABLO   But you'll be back, right?

CHABUCA   No... I don't think so, no. No, I won't... That's why I wanted to let you know. I left you a note at the B&B.

PABLO   Well, I could meet you there, or you could refer me to someone, couldn't you?

CHABUCA   The thing is, something really bad has happened. I can't tell you what exactly, I'm sorry... And well, I have to go.

PABLO   You're lying. Aren't you?

CHABUCA   Excuse me?

PABLO   You're lying.

CHABUCA   No, Pablo.

PABLO   I can tell that you are.

CHABUCA   I'm not, Pablo.

PABLO   Yes, you are. Is this some kind of joke? You think you can go around doing this? You think you can come here, tell me all the things you've told me, fill me with hope and then just disappear? Have you forgotten what we spoke about yesterday?

CHABUCA   No, Pablo, I haven't forgotten.

PABLO   (*Hits the ground with his cane*) Well, it seems that you have. What is wrong with you? What kind of sick game are you playing?

CHABUCA   Please, relax, Pablo. It's not what you think, believe me.

PABLO   What kind of person does something like this?

CHABUCA   I'm sorry, Pablo. I can't tell you. Please don't hurt me. I just can't.

PABLO   What can't you tell me?

CHABUCA   I can't tell you.

PABLO   What is it? (*He hits the ground again, violently*)

CHABUCA   Don't hurt me! What I told you yesterday was the truth. I can't explain. If you want to understand, ask Nela. Leave me alone. I said I can't.

PABLO   Nela? What does Nela have to do with this?

CHABUCA   I can't tell you, Pablo, please don't hurt me!

PABLO   What does Nela have to do with this? (*Slam*) Did you speak to her?

CHABUCA   I can't explain, ask her, please! But don't hurt me. You're scaring me. Please, please don't hurt me. I wanted to do the operation.

PABLO   Have you spoken to her? Have you spoken to her? (*Slam*)

CHABUCA   Don't hurt me. I wanted to do the operation.

PABLO   And you will. You hear me? You will do it.

CHABUCA   Okay, Pablo. Alright. Just don't hurt me.

PABLO   I'm not going to hurt you. Relax. But you're going to go through with what you said.

CHABUCA   Okay. Okay. Please calm down.

PABLO   Let's go.

CHABUCA   Okay.

12. THEY SAY THAT TOMORROW HE WILL BE ABLE TO SEE

Nela *with her Virgin Mary.*

NELA   I'm fed up with everything. I've had enough of Pablo's self-pitying face. Hey, life is tough for all of us. He can stop playing the victim. You know, I'm also blind, in a way. I'm blind to all the things I've never had a chance to see. I'm father-blind, and Japan-blind, I'm blind to all the things I don't know. Mother Mary, he says he's going to have the operation. I'm scared. He says he's going to see. Are you listening? Some woman came along, she says she's an ophthalmologist and that she can cure him. It all happened when I left him alone. But I only left him alone so I could speak with you, Mary. Why do these things happen? I don't want to see it. I don't want to see his eyes seeing me. He's going to kill me if he sees me. Why does everything have to change? Why? I'm not ready. I need things to be still. That's why I love you, Mary. Because you are still. I hate people who say they've seen you cry. Why do they want you to cry? What for? The best thing about you is that you're here, solid and still and made of whatever you're made of, that you're not like us. It's pathetic how easily we fall apart. The best thing about you is that you're here, but you're not really here. If you cried, you'd be just like Pablo, falling apart when he sees again. Right. Now I understand, the Pablo that I love has to be blind forever. And he has to be still, like you. If he starts seeing, then our love will be over. My Pablo is a fool. He's killing us just to see some colours. He's selfish. He's going to regret seeing me. And losing me. It hurts so much. I'm dying inside, Mary. I can't even sing anymore.

13. NICOLÁS

NATALIA   (*Calls* Andrea *by phone*) Hi. Listen, there is one more thing I want to tell you. (*The line cuts*) Hello? Hello? What the hell is going on…? Fucking service. (*Calls customer service*) Hello. (*A recorded message plays on the other end of the line*) Great, a machine… The line is broken… Yes… Yes… I'm not going to hang up until I speak to a human being. (*Someone comes to the line*) Hello, darling. I was in the middle of a very important call when the line cut off, and it's not the first time it's happened. Excuse me? No… no… no… You're going to solve this right now. I'm not hanging up until it's fixed… Well, I don't know, call the manager or… What? Fuck you, that's what my name is. Write it down. Why the hell do you want to know where I live? You're stuck in a basement somewhere in Peru along with twenty other losers and you don't know a thing about Spain. You want to know where I live? In a shit town, in the fucking middle of fucking nowhere, write that down… And your shit company won't let me speak to… someone that… someone that needs me. (*She falls to the ground. Pause*) Sorry, darling. I fell. It's not your fault you have a lousy job where you have to be nice to insane people like me. My name is Natalia. And yours? Nicolás… What a beautiful name… How does it work, Nicolás? You're not allowed to hang up until the customer is satisfied with the service? (*She laughs*) You want to know something? I'd love it if my boyfriend, I mean my ex-boyfriend, I would love it if he had your job. (*Pause*) Hang up… Hang up, Nicolás. (*Sobbing, she throws the phone to the ground*)

14. A MOTHER'S MELODRAMA

Nela *arrives and finds her mother crying on the floor.*

NELA   Mum. Don't cry. When you cry I don't know what to do.

NATALIA   Learn.

NELA   Please, mum. I really don't know what to do.

NATALIA   You don't? What a shame.

NELA   Please, mum.

NATALIA   If you didn't know me, what would you do?

NELA   I don't know… I would hug you. I'd ask you what's wrong.

NATALIA   Okay. Pretend you don't know me.

Nela *hugs her.*

NATALIA   (*Crying harder*) My little one, it's so sad… (*She continues to cry*) Ask me what's wrong!

NELA   What's wrong?

NATALIA   I was thinking about Grandma.

NELA   Really?

NATALIA   Yes. I was thinking about her regret.

NELA   What regret?

NATALIA   Her regret! Grandma Nené had a wart on her forehead, and she called it 'the regret'.

NELA   She never told me that.

NATALIA   Well, she told me. I was stroking her hair one day and at some point, I don't know why, I started stroking her wart, too. That's when she told me.

NELA   Grandma didn't have any warts, mum. (*The two of them hug, both crying*)

NATALIA   Yes, she did, she had one like a little pimple on her forehead. Tiny. And she said to me: 'That's the regret' while I stroked it.

NELA   Are you sure she was talking about the wart?

NATALIA   What else would she be talking about?

NELA   I don't know, something related to whatever you were talking about before.

NATALIA   (*Unsure*) No, I was there and it was obvious. I'm not explaining myself well. But it was obvious that she was saying that the wart was called 'the regret'.

NELA   You're crying because of that, mum?

NATALIA   Who knows! I was thinking about it and then it all came out. Do you always know why you cry? Who knows!

NELA   She never told me about it.

NATALIA   You never saw it. How could she tell you?

NELA   I loved her a lot.

NATALIA   So did I. Actually, now that I think about it, I loved her much more as Grandma Nené than as my own mother. When you were born she became Grandma Nené and everything was much better. Don't have children, Nela. Adopt grandchildren. It's very difficult to be a mother, sometimes you have no idea how to do it. Being a grandmother must be easier. Like a reward after so many years of not knowing.

NELA Mum, I love you.

NATALIA You're so sweet. So silly… When you have a child, I will be a better person and you'll love me more, you'll see.

NELA I love you very much, mum.

NATALIA I know, I love you too. Don't worry… Don't be silly.

NELA Don't be sad.

Natalia *laughs.*

NELA Do you want us to go back to Tucumán?

NATALIA Are you mad? Don't be ridiculous.

NELA You could visit her in the cemetery and bring her flowers.

NATALIA That's nonsense, Nela. Grandma is not at the cemetery. She's dead. She died and that's it… (*Pause*) Why? Do you want to go back to Buenos Aires?

NELA No. Not to Buenos Aires. To Tucumán… sometimes.

NATALIA Really? (*She laughs*)

NELA Yes. Why are you laughing?

NATALIA You were just a child in Tucumán. You wouldn't like it now. It's horrible. Everyone's either very poor or very rich. And guess which group we'd be in.

NELA I do remember. I would like it. It's beautiful. Besides, I don't know, my roots are there. It's my homeland.

NATALIA Your homeland? Stop repeating what you hear! I don't like it! Do you want to have a homeland? (*She grabs a handful of dirt from the soil pile and puts it in* Nela's *hands*) Here, now you have some land of your own. It is yours, because I've given it to you. Nelly, I know I say stupid things sometimes. But Tucumán is very, very far away. You were young and whatever you remember is gone. If you want to travel, go somewhere else. But don't go there. Listen to me: when you leave a place, it's like you cut off a piece of yourself. It's like a wound. Do you understand? Once it is done it's done. It can't disappear. You cut it off and it can heal, but you're still left with a scar. People over there are going to tell you you're from here, and here they'll tell you you're from over there. Which is okay in the end. Because you're not from anywhere.

NELA I don't think that's true.

NATALIA It is. You know where your place is? Where someone loves you. That's where you belong. So if you don't feel loved here, leave. But don't go looking for your roots in Tucumán. Look for someone to love you.

NELA Pablo loves me.

NATALIA Then stay here.

NELA But when he sees me, he won't love me anymore.

NATALIA That means he doesn't love you.

NELA Will he love me when he sees me, mum?

NATALIA I don't know, Nelly. I don't know what goes through a blind man's head. If I were blind, I'd kill myself. I don't know… He looks like a good man. Do you love him?

NELA He makes me happy.

NATALIA Then you love him. Listen, my little sausage, wait to see what happens. If he looks at you intensely, that means he loves you.

NELA What if he doesn't?

NATALIA If he doesn't, he's an idiot. So don't waste your time on him. That would be very sad. The world is full of people. I know it's not working for me, but it will one day, eventually.

Pause.

NELA Shall I get us some tea?

NATALIA When I went to Andrea's house for the first time, the bastard asked me if I wanted some tea. I told him I loved tea. And he said, 'Well, I love thee'.[19] What an idiot.

They both laugh.

NELA I love thee.

NATALIA (*After looking at her for some time*) Come here, sausage. (*She brings* Nela *to her lap*)

Pause.

NATALIA Look at us, we are quite good at being mother and daughter. It's as if I were your grandma.

---

[19] In the original Spanish text, Natalia's comment is a pun, playing on the words *té* ('tea') and *te* (the accusative case of the personal pronoun *tú* ('you'), as in *te quiero* ('I love you')).

15. THE OPERATION

CHABUCA   Have a seat. It's going to hurt quite a bit. You know that, right?

PABLO   I don't care. It's an operation. They always hurt.

CHABUCA   No, I don't mean the operation. It'll hurt afterwards. When you see.

PABLO   I don't care.

CHABUCA   Listen, Pablo. There's something I need to tell you. It's like a non-disclosure agreement that I have with my patients.

PABLO   What do I have to sign?

CHABUCA   Nothing… You have to promise me that you won't say a word about what happened in this room.

PABLO   I don't understand.

CHABUCA   Pablo, I don't operate using traditional methods.

PABLO   What do you mean? Don't frighten me. You said you could cure me.

CHABUCA   I can.

PABLO   Then do it. I don't need to know more. I don't care.

CHABUCA   Do you trust me?

PABLO   Yes.

CHABUCA   Pablo.

PABLO   What!?

CHABUCA   I operate using songs.

PABLO   Using what?

CHABUCA   Anaesthesia. (*She shoves him to the ground*)

The song 'Make Someone Happy' by Jimmy Durante plays as Chabuca *wraps* Pablo's *head with a bandage over his eyes. Meanwhile,* Natalia *packs her suitcase, filling it with dirt that she grabs from the soil pile.* Nela *is praying. The scene lasts as long as the song.*

16. THE LAST SUPPER

Natalia *is sitting on top of her suitcase, smoking.* Nela *enters.*

NELA   Mum, what's happening?

NATALIA   I've invited him to dinner.

NELA   Who?

Pablo *and* Chabuca *appear. Pablo's eyes are still covered in gauze.*

PABLO and CHABUCA: Hello!

NATALIA   Hello. And who is this?

PABLO   My doctor.

CHABUCA   (*Overlapping*) Pablo invited me. But if it's any trouble I'll leave.

NATALIA   As you like.

NELA   (*Overlapping*) Mum! (*She runs away, towards her Virgin*)

PABLO   Nela! Nelly!

NATALIA   Don't you worry about her. She'll be back. Have a seat. What a shit day.

The three of them sit down at the table. An awkward pause. Chabuca *and* Natalia *stare at each other.*

PABLO   Is Nela alright?

NATALIA   She's coming.

NATALIA   (*To* Chabuca) I'm Natalia, Nela's mother. Have a seat, love.

Pause.

NATALIA   Are you a natural redhead?

CHABUCA   Yes.

NATALIA   Ah.

Pause.

CHABUCA   (*Seeing the suitcase*) Are you going on a trip?

PABLO   You're leaving?

NATALIA   No.

Pause.

PABLO   What about Nela?

NATALIA   I told you, she's coming.

CHABUCA   What's in the suitcase?

NATALIA   Stuff.

PABLO   But where is she?

NATALIA   Can't you hear her? She's praying. She's hooked on that absurd religion of hers. If only she were Buddhist or something oriental. But no, of all the possible gods, she chose one made in the image and likeness of man, how sad is that… What a lack of imagination, for God's sake.

CHABUCA   The Bible has some imaginative passages.

NATALIA   I wouldn't know. I don't read best-sellers.

CHABUCA   What's in the suitcase?

NATALIA   My! The doctor is nosy. There's dirt. Dirt, that's what there is.[20]

Natalia *goes to look for* Nela.

NELA   My Holy Mother, don't do this to me. If you're going to bless him with the miracle of sight, make me beautiful or kill me. Make me beautiful or kill me.

NATALIA   Nelaaaaa! Don't you realise we can hear everything? I'm with your guests and I have no fucking idea what to tell them. Can you fucking get your arse over here!

She grabs her by the hair and brings her to the table.

NELA   Hello.

Pause.

NELA   How did the operation go?

CHABUCA   He made me do it, Nela.

NELA   (*To* Pablo) Does it hurt?

PABLO   No.

CHABUCA   (*Overlapping*) Not yet.

NELA   When are you taking his bandages off?

PABLO   Not yet.

CHABUCA   (*Overlapping*) Tomorrow.

NELA   Right.

Pause.

NATALIA   (*To* Nela) Sit down, Nelly. The food is ready…

---

[20] See note 5, p. 23.

CHABUCA   What's for dinner?

NATALIA   I can't believe this woman. (*To* Chabuca) Ciggies. Eat them all.

CHABUCA   What?

PABLO   Cigarettes.

NATALIA   (*Overlapping. Grabs a pack of cigarettes and throws it on the table*) Cigarettes.

Chabuca *lights a cigarette.*

NELA   Mum, enough! (*To* Pablo) Come with me. (*She takes* Pablo *to the back*)

Natalia *and* Chabuca *stare at each other, observing how the other smokes.*

NATALIA   (*To* Chabuca) I feel like shit.

CHABUCA   Me too. I hate the countryside.

NATALIA   So why did you come?

CHABUCA   I don't know. To relax, to connect…

NATALIA   To connect with what?

CHABUCA   I don't know. I thought it would relax me, it would do me good to be here. They told me the countryside was peaceful, and the people laid back. But you're all extremely anxious and there are bugs and creatures everywhere.

NATALIA   Why don't you leave, then?

CHABUCA   I have to wait until his bandages can be taken off.

NATALIA   Will he see?

CHABUCA   He will.

Pause.

NATALIA   Shit.

CHABUCA   Yeah.

17. WHAT HAVE YOUR EYES DONE TO ME

Pablo *is still covered in bandages. As the doctor begins to unwrap them,* Nela *starts covering her own head with bandages. These movements both last as long as the Ada Falcón version of the tango 'Yo no sé que me han hecho tus ojos' ('I Don't Know What Your Eyes Have Done to Me'). By the end of the song,* Nela *is covered up like a mummy and* Pablo *has no bandages left. His eyes are closed. He opens them. He sees.*

18. EPILOGUE: TO MOSCOW

Natalia is dragging out her table; a suitcase is on top of it. She stops when she sees the audience.

NATALIA   I'm leaving this place. This is all very sad. I'm going to Moscow. I took that line from a play.[21] Actually, in the play they never left. Or maybe they went afterwards. After the play finished. But I don't think so. The three girls were very unhappy. I am also very unhappy. But I'm leaving. I'm going to work. They also said that in the play. I could clean houses or something, I don't know. Or maybe I'll sing. I've decided to go somewhere very different. I want to be freezing cold, I want to be out of place until I know what I really want. I want to go somewhere I can't even read the writing. In Moscow the writing looks like little pictures. It's like Japanese writing. I could have chosen Japan, as a matter of fact. Or China. The thing is, I've always thought of Asia as the future, and Russia as the past. I get along better with the past. The past is one's destiny. Among the Muscovites I want to feel lost. Maybe then I will remember where I'm from and I'll know whether I want to go back or not. I don't know if you can understand what I'm saying. Have you ever left a place that felt like it was *yours*? When you leave *that* place you're not from anywhere anymore. And that is actually fine, because there is no such thing as really being from somewhere. But habit is a great deadener. That's a line from another play.[22] Habit is a deadener and makes you believe that what you're used to is yours. That's why leaving is so mind-blowing. It's like hitting a raw nerve. Home doesn't exist. It's just another accident. Home is where your people are. And your people are the ones that you choose, within the possibilities that chance gives you. Nothing is stable, ever, so the only thing you can do is move, move and move until you can latch onto someone or someone latches on to you. At least for a little while. I'm thinking about Andrea. And about Moscow. I'm imagining a frozen river. It's not completely frozen, there are chunks of ice carried by the current. There must be a word for that in Russian. As you must know, people make up the words they need. If you never leave the chunk of ice where you were born, you may well think it doesn't move. But if someone latches on to you, or if you get frightened and jump from one piece to another and another, then you'll realise that all the pieces you left behind are still moving. Everything that is alive moves. And that's when you see this huge ice puzzle in perpetual motion… And you just keep going from piece to piece, looking for a strong one, looking for one that will last.

She puts on a fur hat.

I'm putting on this hat because I'm going to Moscow. And it's cold there. (*Pause*) Nelly died. She fell. They ran over her. She died. It's not right to lose a child. It

---

[21] She is referring to Anton Chekhov's *Three Sisters* (1900).
[22] This is a line from Samuel Beckett's *Waiting for Godot* (1949).

can't be explained. It's a pain that few can understand. It's not like losing a father, or a friend. There are no words for it. See? No one needs that word. It's a strange wound. It hurts in a different way. I don't know. That's why I'm not going to say anything more about this. We never saw Pablo again. The operation was a success. He began to see, and he left. We didn't see him again. Chabuca also left town. We're all leaving this place. Everybody leaves small towns. Except for the old people, who couldn't get out in time. Or the people who are 'at one with nature', those tree-huggers. No, I'm not one of them. No. (*Pause*) What I want to say is, it hurts all over. It hurts here (*she touches her forehead*), here (*she touches her sternum*) and it hurts here, too (*she touches her knee*). But I'm not going to quit smoking. And I'm certainly not going to stop moving until I find a comfortable chunk of ice.

Suddenly, she sees the moon.

Oh my God! What a beautiful moon!

Pause.

I'm looking at the moon.

Pause.

My mother would be singing now.

She chuckles. She sings.

Ma che luna...
ma che luna c'è stasera
vede er monno chi s'affaccia a 'sta ringhiera
da San Pietro all'artre cupole laggiù

fino ar mare più lontano sempre più.
Che m'importa se quassù non c'è nessuno
che m'importa si nun trovo da scaglia'
mo' sti fiori li regalo a' Roma bella
che li porti ad un sordato
in sentinella.[23]

---

[23] 'What a moon... | What a beautiful moon there is tonight. | If I look out on this railing, I can see the whole world at my feet, | From Saint Peter's Basilica to the smaller domes of the city, | All the way to the sea and farther and farther away. | What do I care if there is nobody up here, | What do I care if there is nobody down there to catch them, | I throw these flowers out to the beautiful city of Rome. | Let the city bring them to a soldier | Waiting out on his night shift.' This excerpt is from the Italian song 'Com'è bello far l'amore quando è sera' ('Oh how beautiful it is to make love when the sun goes down'), sung by the actress Anna Magnani in the film *We, the Women* (1953). In the original production of *The Eyes* Anna Magnani was an important referent in the preparation of Natalia's character.

Pause.

She takes off her fur hat. She looks for a cigarette, puts it in her mouth, looks for her lighter and cannot find it.

(*To the audience*) Does anyone have a light?

She sits down once again on the suitcase.

Blackout.

AN INTERVIEW WITH PABLO MESSIEZ
(Alma Prelec)

This interview was originally carried out in December 2021 and subsequently revised with Pablo Messiez.

ALMA PRELEC   In several interviews you have mentioned that *The Eyes* came together during a difficult period in your life, which in turn impacted its creation. Could you reconstruct this moment?

PABLO MESSIEZ   I moved to Spain on 3 December 2008, trying to salvage a relationship that was falling apart. Within two months of my arrival, we separated. At the time I was holding rehearsals for *Muda* ['Mute'], my first directorial project in Spain, and I was searching for ideas for new projects. By chance I came across Pérez Galdós's *Marianela* in a second-hand bookshop. Something about the way in which Galdós deals with the essence of Madrid has always intrigued me, so when I saw the book, I decided to leaf through it. I thought it was a nice coincidence that the protagonist and I had the same name, and that Marianela's character was nicknamed Nela — just like the lead actress in *Muda*, Marianela Pensado. So I decided to buy it. What struck me, reading it, were the questions it raised about love and about differing points of view: what one thinks about oneself and about a relationship, and what others tell us that they see from the outside.

Both the project and the creation of its characters were heavily influenced by the cast. To give just one example, I had collaborated with the actress Fernanda Orazi in *Muda*. During that process we had understood each other very well in exploring registers linked to comedy, but I soon realised that Fernanda had enormous potential to explore other zones and genres. And that is what we did in *The Eyes*. In the end the work with Fernanda determined the characterisation of Natalia, the mother.

AP   You often create a production through devising with actors. Did you have the cast for *The Eyes* decided before beginning?

PM   I almost always begin with actors — in my work it is above all the cast that determines the dramaturgy. I staged *The Eyes* with the same cast as *Muda* (Violeta Pérez, who played Chabuca, was the only exception). There were also, obviously, material limitations, in the sense that I couldn't set my sights on staging all the characters that appear in Galdós's *Marianela*. If I'm to be perfectly honest, however, I also wasn't particularly interested in doing so. What I wanted was to take the story of Marianela and Pablo and rework it with the group of actors that I had.

AP How would you situate the production within your overall trajectory?

PM *The Eyes* represented an important moment for me. It was the first play that I staged in Spain in which I questioned what I wanted to do as a director. *Muda* had been my Spanish premiere, and it was still contaminated with those elements that Spanish audiences have come to expect from contemporary Argentine theatre. Or, at least, with the elements I thought they expected: a 'living room' play, with a very simple spatial design; the focus is on the actors' performances.

From *The Eyes* onwards, however, I became interested in the specifically theatrical — that is to say, not only the work with actors and the given circumstances of a play, but also with the role of time and space within the theatre. For example, there is a very long monologue in *The Eyes*, and to stop the action with that text, which functions as a sort of aria, is to think about theatre in terms of time and space. That moment is of a completely different nature compared to the rest of the play, and it only makes sense because of what the actor does with those words and how she embodies them.

On the other hand, my approach also changed in terms of valuing the imperfect, the unfinished, and of distancing myself from a text-focused understanding of theatre. In *Muda* one can still discern the intention to stage a 'well-written' play: it has a classic theatrical structure from the outset, and a clear central conflict and denouement (with a final twist). By contrast, the logic that sustains *The Eyes* is not dramaturgical in the classical sense, but rather it is intimately associated with what happens on stage. It is for this reason that I initially rejected the offer to publish the play. I hadn't worked on it as a literary creation, as something independent from the production itself. My texts were 'pre-texts'. The point of them was to generate what would take place on stage and, when the production was over, they would stay there merely as testimony to what happened. That is why I entitled my first volume, *Las palabras de las obras* ['The Words from the Plays']. I wanted to emphasise that they were not plays, but simply the words that were said on stage.

AP In relation to this, what did you bring with you from Argentina, as a creator, and what did you encounter in Spain? What do you believe are the main differences between the two theatrical systems?

PM The greatest difference is that of financial resources, which obviously ends up having an aesthetic impact. The norm in Argentina is precarity; it is what is expected. Productions are not thought through in terms of the available budget, but simply from the will to stage them. The advantage in this is that the link with the work is pure; it is sustained by a need that gives meaning to everything. The negative aspect is that the role of the set and design ends up being put to one side, as this would imply engaging with a theatrical logic that requires money. There is also something perverse in a system that sees precarity as the norm. When I lived in Argentina, twelve years ago, I was used to working like this. Even when you had established a name for yourself and could begin to convince a sponsor to finance your play (that is to say, even when there was money involved), rehearsal pay, for example, was not included in the production expenses.

When I arrived to Madrid, I found the complete opposite. Work was extremely regulated: if there was no money there could in turn be no rehearsals. But at the same time this also implied that if you received a grant, you had to, in some way, justify this financial investment. The situation now is much more precarious, as it is in Buenos Aires. This has had an impact on production models. In recent years, for example, a number of small alternative theatres have popped up in Spain.

AP   What did Spain offer you, apart from the possibility of working with a bigger budget?

PM   It's not just the money. As a director, having financial support allows you to materialise those ideas that you first imagined — such as, for example, a space covered in soil like the one in *The Eyes* (an idea that would be too expensive within an Argentine context). And, of course, knowing that I would have the space I had imagined impacted the whole work. As did the fact that rehearsals were paid. Making a living from theatre changes your relationship to the activity. Until a few years after I moved to Spain, I had never been able to make a living from theatre. In Argentina I had to supplement my income with other jobs; I worked in cultural management, for the Tango, Film and Theatre Festivals in Buenos Aires. This experience in cultural management (I also worked for the Festival de Otoño in Madrid) was of significant help. It helped me to not have a romantic idea of creation, and to take into account the means of production: what could and what could not be done.

AP   It's curious, isn't it, that in a country in which theatre practitioners cannot make a living, there has been such an explosion of talent.

PM   Yes, in Argentina one can observe a truly special relationship to the theatre, and also to training. There are schools of excellent acting maestros who people train with as though they were going to the gym, which is not the case in Spain, or at least not as much. It's a very powerful bond, and a passionate one as well.

AP   How would you explain this?

PM   I don't know because it's not as if there is an incentive coming from the government, as might be the case in Germany or the UK. It's not that it's valued. It's mentioned when it's politically convenient to say that Argentine theatre is good, but in terms of cultural policy it is not exactly one of the most cared-for areas.

AP The Quintero brothers adapted *Marianela* for the stage, and there have been several film versions of the text too. Were you familiar with them?

PM My first encounter with the story was through Galdós. It was only later that I saw the Argentine film from 1955 (because I love Olga Zubarry, the actress) and the Spanish film from 1972, with Rocío Durcal. In any case, I took the novel as a starting point and then forgot about it. I wouldn't say that *The Eyes* is an adaptation of *Marianela*, although Linda Willem, a North American scholar who has worked on staged versions of Galdós's work, does think it is.

AP When you engage in re-writing you tend to pick narrative texts (apart from Galdós, you have worked with novels by Manuel Puig, Samantha Schweblin and Carson McCullers…), and in the introduction to *Las palabras de las obras* you state that your plays are based on the novels that you never wrote (Messiez 2017, 11). What role does narrative occupy in your theatrical work?

PM Well, it's not only novels that I freely adapt; in my staging of García Lorca's *Blood Wedding*, for example, we also reworked much of the second act. I think the need to adapt is related to the material from which I am starting and how time has affected it. With both a novel and a play, I see the text as a pretext. One has to work with the material in the same way that one works with space and time, that is to say, with absolute freedom, paying attention to how it will work with the bodies speaking the text and how it resonates in a determined present moment.

That said, I love reading novels and short stories, and sometimes I do encounter texts that challenge me as a director. When that happens, it's true that working across media requires you to think about the text in a way that doesn't occur when you're working with a play. What I mean here is that a novel doesn't carry in itself the stain of another artistic form. Adapting a text to the stage demands that one answers the question of why it was necessary to do so in the first place, why adapt something that already works just as it is. I find this exercise very stimulating, as it ends up being a reflection about what theatre really is.

AP Do you believe, then, that working with narrative text, where adaptation is always necessary, gives you more artistic freedom?

PM Yes, although that freedom is also relative, especially in the case of living authors who can tell you that they don't like your idea. My first production, *Antes* ['Before'], was based on Carson McCullers's novel *The Member of the Wedding*. I wrote to McCullers's agent asking for the rights, noting that in my version I only wished to stage three characters from the original text. The first thing the agent said to me was that an adaptation by McCullers already existed, and when I tried to explain that I wanted to do something different, she directly denied me the rights. That 'no' ended up conditioning the dramaturgy of the play. I managed to find out that if the original novel appeared as a citation or as an intertextual reference, then I wouldn't need the rights. So that is what we did: in the piece, the characters made all references to the text explicit, and that is how we managed to stage it.

AP   You staged *The Eyes*, a play about blindness, after staging *Muda*. Why the recurrent exploration of senses and their absence?

PM   To be honest, purely by chance, and after all, at the end of the day the character in *Muda* is not actually mute. It's true, however, that this play is the first to deal with the question of perspectives, a topic now recurrent in my work. I am drawn to the idea of how difficult it is to see and how much is omitted in what we see. This is not unlike what happens on a physiological level: a healthy eye, in order to see, also needs a blind spot. I think this is a good metaphor for a point of view: to have one you must avoid considering others. For me, this is the great human (and theatrical) question — we need to understand each other, but to understand each other the basic starting point is to remember that beliefs are perspectives that by definition avoid others.

AP   You are a reflective creator, you are constantly reading essays and theory, and you often stage what has impacted you as a reader. What were you reading when you created *The Eyes*?

PM   Roland Barthes's *A Lover's Discourse: Fragments*, which is named in the play. I also read Eduardo del Estal's *Historia de la mirada* ['History of the Gaze'] and, if I recall correctly, it was back then when I also read *The Mind's Eye* by Oliver Sacks, although I don't think this last text had much weight in the end.

AP   In several interviews you've mentioned that you don't like didactic theatre, or plays that try to send out a message. Still, your plays often include monologues or extensive speeches in which the author's voice can be discerned (perhaps because you are self-reflective as a creator).

PM   Yes, absolutely. In fact, I think this tendency bothers me because I know that I have been guilty of it. As I have developed as a playwright, I have tried to be more and more precise. Natalia has an enormous monologue in *The Eyes*: at this point I wouldn't necessarily take it out, but I would re-consider it. That is something that I did later, in *Todo el tiempo del mundo* ['All the Time in the World']. The latter also has a very long monologue, which is full of various ideas, but what happens on stage questions and frustrates what the text says. It's a monologue that is nourished by a repeated phrase, 'mañana nazco' ['tomorrow I will be born'], but what the character says is never materialised: in the end, the character is not born. That is to say, the idea remains in balance, it oscillates between one possibility and another. Although I should add that many reviews didn't like this contradiction. They would have preferred the play to end in a more satisfying way. But asking theatre to provide neat endings is nonsense.

AP Yes, well in any case in the final monologue in *The Eyes* Natalia breaks the fourth wall by asking the audience for a light, which in a way invites a dialogue rather than imposes an idea, right?

PM Yes, yes.

AP This is one of many moments in the play in which you expose the artificial nature of theatre. Why do you use this device so often in your productions?

PM Theatre often ignores the fact that there is an audience, as though the theatrical situation would fracture if its structure (a group of people looking at a stage) were revealed. The encounter between the audience's gaze, the set, and what is happening on it is precisely where the theatrical lives. And the thing is that the audience doesn't only give the production its final reading, but also its opening. Until the public arrives there is no play, and as soon as the audience's gaze is fixed on the stage, the play has begun — even if, for one reason or another, the actor does not come out on stage.

I don't believe exposing artifice weakens theatre; I believe it makes it stronger. In my case the use of metatheatre is also a response, perhaps a slightly reactive one, to a type of theatre that adopts a naïve position to the spectator's 'suspension of disbelief'. Someone's phone goes off in the audience and the actors and spectators pretend it isn't happening, when in truth it is very easy to incorporate any eventuality like this into the play itself, on any given day. Theatre must nourish itself from whatever occurs in the moment of encounter with the audience.

AP What role does improvisation play in the production? There is an entire scene set to music, the moment that Pablo and Nela dance, and this is left to be improvised.

PM The work in the moment you are referencing was very physical, and that was why I wanted them to improvise, but I do not generally use improvisation as a device. The remainder of the production is extremely scripted.

AP And what about the visual references? The scene in which Natalia is on the phone to her ex-partner reminded me of Anna Magnani in Roberto Rossellini's film version of Jean Cocteau's *The Human Voice*.

PM Yes, absolutely, for example Fernanda's wrapping the telephone cord around her is an homage to the film. The final song is taken from another film with Anna Magnani, *We, the Women* (1953). In the stage design there are also echoes of Pina Bausch's use of dirt in *The Rite of Spring*, a show that has always impacted me greatly.

AP The set design, specifically the use of soil on the ground, became charged with meaning whenever the characters would mention their homelands, but it also literally affected the actors, in that they would end the performance with their faces smeared with dirt.

PM Yes, as I said, space occupied a fundamental role in *The Eyes*, as it hadn't done in any of my previous works. Not only did it literally stain the actors, but it also affected how they moved. The dirt created a sense of instability. It told the story of being constantly on the move, in search of equilibrium (so present in the case of Natalia, who is in a state of perpetual exile), and at the same time it reminded the audience of how theatre engages with space.

AP And the kitsch detail of the statue of the Virgin with a doll's head?

PM Oh, that is another visual reference that I forgot to mention. Lucrecia Martel's *La ciénaga* was very present when it came to imagining Nela. It's a vision of religion, but from the popular point of view. Nela's faith, at the end of the day, has a pagan element to it: she invents her own version of the Virgin. She gives her such a realness that when what she has begged for doesn't take place, she feels betrayed, and she complains to the statue, as though it were a real person. There is something very beautiful in faith, in that necessity of believing that there is something more out there. In fact, this is something I explored in my piece *La voluntad de creer* ['The Will to Believe'].

AP In Natalia's final monologue there is an explicit homage to Chekhov's *Three Sisters*, a play that seems to run through your career. What draws you to it?

PM Fate has placed it in front of me at several points in my life. Inda Ledesma's 1987 version, which premiered at the San Martín Theatre in Buenos Aires, was one of the first plays I ever saw. It made me realise I wanted to work in theatre. It is also the play that brought me to Spain for the first time as an actor (I was playing Natasha in Daniel Veronese's version, *Un hombre que se ahoga* ['A Man Who Drowns']). It remains very present in my work. It was an important source of inspiration for *Las canciones* ['The Songs'], one of my most recent pieces. One day, perhaps, I will create a version that is closer to Chekhov's original play.

It's a play that is profoundly theatrical, in that it is told from the perspective of time and of space — elements at the heart of theatre. The play tells the story of the expulsion of three sisters, the first act begins in the living room, the second, in a small room, and the third, in the garden. And meanwhile Natasha gains more and more territory in their house.

AP Chabuca is a character who, like Natasha, does not have much text, but even so is able to destabilise everything.

PM Yes, that's right. Chabuca is an outsider: she arrives with a foreign logic and perspective about what is going on. That is what is also fascinating in *Three Sisters*, that clash of perspectives that is also and above all a clash between classes, between rich intellectuals and a middle-class woman who needs to keep her child out of a humid room. I sense that sometimes the play is read from a slightly snobbish perspective, one which sees Natasha as a ridiculous person, but the truth is that Natasha's requests are well-founded and not at all ridiculous.

AP   To continue with the theme of references and influences, your earlier work continues to leave its marks on your current projects. For example, the phrase 'It hurts here, and here, and here', which helped to situate the actor in the body of the character in *The Eyes*, appears again in *Los brillantes empeños* ('Brilliant Endeavours', 2014); similarly, Natalia's mother (Grandma Nené) is also there in *Todo el tiempo del mundo* (2016).

PM   Let's say that my plays are, in a way, the re-writing of one same text. I think this is a response to my conscious search for a style. There is a Deleuze quote that I like very much: 'style is the economy of language'.[1] I am interested in this idea of refining one's relationship with words until finding a voice, or a way of telling a story. Sometimes things appear in a play that I really like, and it saddens me when they disappear after the production is over. We cannot forget that theatre is ephemeral; it is born and dies in each performance. So, if later on, while working on a new production, I realise that a segment that I previously liked would fit in, I include it again.

AP   In the future, would you like to re-stage any of your previous works?

PM   It depends on the text. Beckett's *Happy Days* and Lorca's *Blood Wedding*, yes, because they are immense works. A play that has stood the test of time contains in itself a mystery that invites one to explore. I am less interested in the idea of restaging contemporary plays. I was recently asked to direct again Alberto Conejero's *La piedra oscura* ['The Dark Stone'], this time in Argentina, and I declined. I wouldn't stage one of my own plays again either; returning to one's own material is to return to speak with oneself and that is not appealing to me. Especially because I think of each play as part of one same fabric, so I prefer to open up my imagination to see what new ideas might appear. But, then again, never say never.

AP   In the title you define *The Eyes* as a 'telluric melodrama' and one of the scenes is also called 'a mother's melodrama'. In an interview about *Todo*

---

[1] 'When a language is so strained that it starts to stutter, or to murmur and stammer [...] *then language in its entirety reaches the limit* that marks its outside and makes it confront silence. When a language is strained in this way, language in its entirety is submitted to a pressure that makes it fall silent. Style — the foreign language within language — is made up of these two operations; or should we instead speak with Proust of a non-style, that is, of "the elements of a style to come which do not yet exist"? Style is the economy of language. To make one's language stutter, face to face, or face to back, and at the same time to push language as a whole to its limit, to its outside, to its silence — this would be like the *boom* and the *crash*' (Deleuze 1998, p. 113).

el tiempo del mundo you said that you work a lot with 'comic melodrama' (Montenegro 2016). Why this obsession with melodrama?

PM   I like the idea that theatre is a space of extremes, of the extra-quotidian, and melodrama is an extreme mode of viewing human relations. As I said before, with *The Eyes* I tried to separate myself from what was expected from Argentine theatre. One of those changes, for example, was to set aside a type of realist-traditionalist form of expression that rejects screams or exaggerated gestures. And the 'mother's melodrama' as a cinematographic motif has always fascinated me.

AP   The presence of songs in your productions is very characteristic of your work (*Las canciones* is perhaps the most complete expression of this exploration with music).[2] In *The Eyes* the songs appear during transitions, they intervene in the action, they give titles to the scenes, sometimes they are the scene itself… Could you tell us a bit more about how these songs were introduced into the production?

PM   Well, here we return to the idea of melodrama, a 'drama of music'. Almost all the songs were there from the beginning. Incorporating Ada Falcón's *Yo no sé qué me han hecho tus ojos* ['I Don't Know What Your Eyes Have Done to Me'] was a given. I was also going to include a song by Nina Simone, but I couldn't get the rights to it, so in the end I decided to introduce a different one: *He Needs Me. Acércate, cholito* ['Come Closer, *Cholito*'] appeared later during a rehearsal, but it ended up being fundamental to the construction of Chabuca's character, who originally was neither Peruvian, nor was called Chabuca Granda (I liked the name because of how it sounded). In my case the process of writing goes through fits and starts; there is no pre-planned logic.

AP   Poetry is another of your passions. There is a scene in *The Eyes* when Pablo recites a poem by E. E. Cummings for Nela. How did this idea come about and what role does it play in the production?

PM   The actress who plays Nela has very small hands, and if I remember correctly, the poem came about because of that association. Apart from being one of the most beautiful poems that I know, the content matched the play very well as it spoke about the idea of perspective. On the other hand, I also liked it as a tool for exploring tempo and the act of listening. A composition that has a clear rhythm ends up taking over at a certain moment in time; it creates a sort of suspension that has an impact on whoever is hearing it. In a way, this impact is maintained even after the poem is over. This is something that I explored in depth in *Las canciones*.

---

[2] Premiered in 2019, the play explores an encounter between a group of people listening to a diverse array of music, and how this music changes them.

AP Could you discuss the characters' different accents?

PM I was interested in their musicality, obviously, but also in working with the idea of Nela and Natalia's successive exiles. I wanted this exile to be complex, so that there wasn't just one place that was longed for. When the past is a reality that is traversed by nomadism, to yearn for a space is to yearn for a time that has passed. And so, the confrontation of the accents in the play tells the story of the mother-daughter conflict: Natalia speaks in the way that is spoken in the place where she wants to live (that is to say, Buenos Aires), while she rejects her native Tucumán. Nela, by contrast, uses her accent to assert her sense of belonging to that land. At the same time, Natalia (whose name was inspired by Natalia Ginzburg) is also linked to Italy. In the play, Italy is one of the many lands (and identities) 'in tension'.

AP You created *The Eyes* with the actors, which also constitutes another layer of difficulty when it comes to working with a new team. What would you say to the actors and director of a possible future staging of this play in English?

PM I would tell them to explore the text freely; I would prefer to be kept in the dark and to be surprised on the day of the premiere. The most beautiful thing for an author is to discover all the possibilities that a text can offer. There have been two further stagings of *The Eyes* apart from my own: one in Mexico and another in Greece. I don't speak any Greek, but the performance was very good indeed. It was much darker, both metaphorically and literally (the lighting design was much dimmer). It moved me to discover the potential of this play, to see how it could resonate in another culture.

AP We have to admit that we feel that in English the characters are different to those in the Spanish text.

PM Yes, reading it I also found that it sounded different. In fact, while I was reading your translation, I couldn't help imagining it like one of Mike Leigh's films from the nineties era (*Secrets and Lies* was an important reference for *Muda*). That's fine. Languages are impregnated with ideologies and character typologies; when you change the language different features immediately appear.

BIBLIOGRAPHY

Anderson, Andrew A. 2015. 'Necessary Sacrifices: From Romanticism to Naturalism in Galdós' *Marianela*', *Bulletin of Spanish Studies*, 92.6, pp. 907–29, doi:10.1080/14753820.2014.947849
Arlt, Roberto. 1942. 'Pequeña historia del Teatro del Pueblo', *Conducta*, 21 <https://ahira.com.ar/ejemplares/conducta-n-21/> [accessed 10 January 2024]
Bartís, Ricardo. 2003. *Cancha con niebla* (Atuel)
Battezzati, Santiago. 2019. 'Breve historia de un modo de producción en el teatro alternativo en Buenos Aires', *Latin American Theatre Review*, 53.1, pp. 5–22, doi:10.1353/ltr.2019.0019
—— 2018. 'Aprendiendo a lo largo de la ciudad: la carrera de los estudiantes de actuación en Buenos Aires', *Revista humanidades*, 8.2, pp. 1–33, doi:10.15517/h.v8i2.33339
Bayardo García, Rubén. 1997. *El teatro 'off Corrientes': ¿una alternativa estético-cultural?* (unpublished PhD thesis, Universidad de Buenos Aires) <http://repositorio.filo.uba.ar/handle/filodigital/2931> [accessed 30 May 2024]
Bresson, Robert. 1986. *Notes on the Cinematographer* (Quartet Books)
CEPAL. 2016. *Territorio y desarrollo en la Argentina: las brechas estructurales de desarrollo en la provincia de Tucumán* (Cepal. Nacionaes Unidas) <http://hdl.handle.net/11362/40836> [accessed 10 January 2024]
Chillida, Eduardo. 2005. *Escritos* (Blow Up)
Ciller, Carmen. 2016. 'The Influence of Argentine Acting Schools in Spain from the 1980s', in Dean Allbritton, Alejandro Melero and Tom Whittaker (eds), *Performance and Spanish Film* (Manchester University Press, 2016), pp. 110–21
Cornago, Oscar. 2006. 'Teatralidades barrocas en Argentina y España (en torno a Ricardo Bartís)', *Teatro XXI*, 21, pp. 18–24 <http://archivoartea.uclm.es/textos/teatralidades-barrocas-en-argentina-y-espana-en-torno-a-ricardo-bartis> [accessed 10 January 2024]
Cotilla Vaca, Marcelino. 2013. 'Omisión de palabra y otras rupturas en el teatro de Claudio Tolcachir análisis pragmalingüístico y estético', in C. Reverte Bernal (coord.), *Diálogos culturales en la literatura iberoamericana: Actas del XXXIX Congreso del Instituto Internacional de Literatura Iberoamericana* (Verbum), pp. 1440–51
Dansilio, María Florencia. 2017. *La théâtralité retrouvée Étude socio-esthétique du théâtre indépendant à Buenos Aires (1983-2003)* (partially unpublished PhD thesis, Université Sorbonne Paris Cité / Université Sorbonne Nouvelle Paris 3) <https://theses.hal.science/tel-01914226> [accessed 10 January 2024]
De Mauro, Karina. 2011. *La técnica de actuación en Buenos Aires. Elementos para un modelo de análisis de la actuación teatral a partir del caso porteño* (partially unpublished PhD thesis, Universidad de Buenos Aires) <http://repositorio.filo.uba.ar/handle/filodigital/1351> [accessed 10 January 2024]
—— 2018. 'Entre el mundo del arte y el mundo del trabajo. Herramientas conceptuales para comprender la dimensión laboral del trabajo artístico',

Telondefondo. Revista De Teoría Y Crítica Teatral, 14.27, pp. 114–43, doi:10.34096/tdf.n27.5097

Deleuze, Gilles. 1998. *Essays: Critical and Clinical* (Verso)

—— 2003. *Francis Bacon: The Logic of Sensation* (Continuum)

DeMaria, Laura. 2014. *Buenos Aires y las provincias. Relatos para desarmar* (Viterbo)

Dubatti, Jorge. 2012. *Cien años de teatro argentino* (Biblos)

Encuesta Nacional de Consumos Culturales. 2022. *Encuesta Nacional de Consumos Culturales*, Sistema de Información Cultural de la Argentina / Ministerio de Cultura Presidencia de la Nación <https://www.sinca.gob.ar/Encuestas.aspx> [accessed 10 January 2024]

Ferreyra, Sandra. 2019. *Estética de lo inefable. Hacia una genealogía materialista del teatro argentino* (Ediciones UNGS)

Fukelman, María. 2017. 'Un recorrido por el Teatro del Pueblo, primer teatro independiente de Buenos Aires', in P. Alonso, M. Fukelman, B. Girotti and J. Trombetta (eds), *Teatro independiente: historia y actualidad* (Ediciones del CCC), pp. 47–66 <https://repositorio.uca.edu.ar/handle/123456789/4788> [accessed 10 January 2024]

Graham Jones, Jean. 2014. 'Anticipated Failure, or Translating Rafael Spregelburd's Play into English', *Symposium: A Quarterly Journal in Modern Literatures*, 68.3, pp. 135–46, doi:10.1080/00397709.2014.938985

Kessler, Gabriel, and M. M. Di Virgilio. 2010. 'Impoverishment of the Middle Class in Argentina: The "New Poor" in Latin America', *Laboratorium*, 2.3, pp. 210–20 <https://www.soclabo.org/index.php/laboratorium/article/view/202> [accessed 10 January 2024]

La Caja del Apuntador. 2011. 'Los Ojos', La Caja del Apuntador, RTVE <https://www.rtve.es/play/audios/la-caja-del-apuntador/caja-del-apuntador-ojos-teatro-fernan-gomez-madrid-20-11-11/1254022/> [accessed 30 May 2024]

Larra, Raúl. 1978. *Leónidas Barletta. El hombre de la campana* (Conducta)

La Vanguardia. 2020. 'El Teatro Alhambra presenta la obra *Los Mariachis*, escrita y dirigida por Pablo Remón', *La Vanguardia*, 12 March <https://www.lavanguardia.com/local/sevilla/20200312/474099929548/el-teatro-alhambra-presenta-la-obra-los-mariachis-escrita-y-dirigida-por-pablo-remon.html> [accessed 10 January 2024]

Messiez, Pablo. 2017. *Las palabras de las obras* (Continta me tienes)

—— 2019. *El tiempo que estemos juntos y algunas notas sobre actuación* (Continta me tienes)

Molina, Javier. 2012. 'Making Drama Out of a Crisis — and a Dilapidated Madrid Apartment', *El País. English Edition*, 19 July <https://english.elpais.com/elpais/2012/07/19/inenglish/1342697131_147616.html> [accessed 10 January 2024]

Montenegro, María. 2016. 'Es extraño creer que la realidad es algo más que una construcción de palabras', *Diagonal*, 22 November <https://www.diagonalperiodico.net/culturas/32391-entrevista-pablo-messiez-estreno-teatro-todo-tiempo-del-mundo.html> [accessed 5 October 2024]

Ordóñez, Marcos. 2011. 'Arácnida en tu pelo', *El País*, 3 December <https://elpais.com/diario/2011/12/03/babelia/1322874783_850215.html> [accessed 10 January 2024]

Pellettieri, Osvaldo (dir.). 2003. *Historia del teatro argentino en Buenos Aires. La segunda modernidad (1949–1976)* (Galerna)

—— 2006. *Teatro del Pueblo: una utopía concretada* (Galerna)
Peretti, Diego. 2016. 'Mauricio Kartún', *Monstruos* (Canal Encuentro), YouTube <https://www.youtube.com/watch?v=6T5eEuBK94A> [accessed 5 October 2023]
Pérez Galdós, Benito. 2001. *Marianela* (Biblioteca Virtual Miguel de Cervantes)
Públicos de teatro. 2020. *Públicos de teatro. Perfiles y hábitos entre los espectadores de teatro independiente en la Ciudad de Buenos Aires* (Alternativa Teatral, Enfoque de Consumos Culturales, Instituto Nacional del Teatro) <https://www.alternativateatral.com/docs/publicos%20teatro%20_vf_alternativa_enfoque-06-2020.pdf> [accessed 10 January 2024]
Ramírez de Haro, Íñigo. 2006. 'Increíble pero cierto. Relaciones entre el teatro argentino y español en la actualidad', in *Dos escenarios. Intercambio teatral entre España y Argentina* (Galerna), pp. 211–18
Rimoldi, Lucas. 2015. 'La antología de literatura dramática. Características y manifestaciones en Argentina desde 1981 a la actualidad', *BSS*, 92.1, pp. 107–29, doi:10.1080/14753820.2014.942568
—— 2019. 'Estudio longitudinal de la representación social del teatro en una cohorte de 25 dramaturgos argentinos de entre 35 y 45 años', *Moderna språk*, 113.1, pp. 243–62, doi:10.58221/mosp.v113i1.7657
Rimoldi, Lucas, and Mónica Monchietti. 2016. 'Una cohorte de artistas gestores', *Taller de Letras*, 59, pp. 111–23, doi:10.7764/tl59111-123
Romo, Juan Luis. 2019. 'Pablo Messiez: "Prefiero armar espectáculos que programaciones"', *El Mundo*, 9 April <https://www.elmundo.es/metropoli/teatro/2019/04/09/5cac88aefc6c83aa1d8b46b9.html> [accessed 10 January 2024]
Rozenholc, Alejandro. 2015. *Análisis de los subsidios públicos otorgados a las cooperativas de teatro y a las salas o espacios teatrales pertenecientes al circuito de producción alternativo de la Ciudad Autónoma de Buenos Aires. Los casos del Fondo Nacional de las Artes, el Instituto Proteatro y el Instituto Nacional del Teatro durante el período 2000-2010* (unpublished MA thesis, Universidad de Buenos Aires) <http://bibliotecadigital.econ.uba.ar/econ/collection/tpos/document/1502-0204_RozenholcA> [accessed 10 January 2024]
Salvatierra Capdevila, Carmina. 2013. 'Las nuevas tendencias del teatro argentino en el teatro catalán', in M. Gonzalo Rodríguez and M. Sikora (eds), *Representaciones y acontecimientos* (Galerna), pp. 69–78
Saura-Clares, Alba. 2021. 'La poética escénica de Pablo Messiez: el montaje de *Los días felices*', *Bulletin of Spanish Studies*, 98.8, doi:10.1080/14753820.2021.1971409
Scherer, Karina. 2016, *Análisis de la Dinámica de Intercambio de Proyectos Teatrales entre Buenos Aires y Madrid durante el período 2008-2015* (unpublished MA thesis, Universidad de Buenos Aires) <http://bibliotecadigital.econ.uba.ar/download/tpos/1502-1039_SchererKB.pdf> [accessed 10 January 2024]
SINCA. n.d. 'En la Argentina hay más de 1.500 salas de teatro' <https://www.sinca.gob.ar/VerNoticia.aspx?Id=35> [accessed 10 January 2024]
Solé, Joan. 2021. 'Pablo Messiez i Fernanda Orazi', Area 44/45 episode 5, *Revista Pausa* <https://www.revistapausa.cat/podcast> [accessed 10 January 2024]
Svampa, Maristella. 2005. *La sociedad excluyente. La Argentina bajo el signo del neoliberalismo* (Taurus)
Sylvester, David. 1999. *The Brutality of Fact: Interviews with Francis Bacon* (Thames and Hudson)

Taylor, Diana. 1997. *Disappearing Acts: Spectacles of Gender and Nationality* (Duke University Press)

Teatroteca, n.d. <http://teatroteca.teatro.es/opac> [accessed 10 January 2024]

Tirri, Néstor. 1973. *Realismo y teatro argentino* (Ediciones La Bastilla)

Tortosa, Mauro. 2021. '¡Quiero ser actriz! Jóvenes talentos pelean por unas pocas plazas en centros públicos frente a un sistema universitario elitista', *Infolibre*, 28 February <https://www.infolibre.es/politica/quiero-actriz-jovenes-talentos-pelean-plazas-centros-publicos-frente-sistema-universitario-elitista_1_1193500.html> [accessed 10 January 2024]

Villarreal, Alberto. 2019. 'Daniel Veronese en conversación con Alberto Villarreal', Cátedra Ingmar Bergman UNAM, YouTube <https://www.youtube.com/watch?v=PKNexmKxMTI> [accessed 10 January 2024]

Werth, Brenda. 2010. 'Embodying the Middle Class in Argentine Theater under Neoliberalism', *GESTOS: Revista de teoría y práctica de teatro hispánico*, 50, pp. 141–58

Willem, Linda. 2018. 'Writing and Adapting Disability: Galdós' *Marianela* and Pablo Messiez's *Los ojos*', *Bulletin of Spanish Studies*, 95.9–10, pp. 109–20, doi:10.1080/14753820.2018.1534796

Yaccar, María Daniela. 2024. 'La Ley Bases excluye una posible disolución, pero hay otros riesgos', *Página 12*, 14 June <https://www.pagina12.com.ar/744474-la-ley-bases-excluye-una-posible-disolucion-pero-hay-otros-r> [accessed 4 October 2024]

MODERN HUMANITIES RESEARCH ASSOCIATION
NEW TRANSLATIONS

A SELECTION OF RECENTLY PUBLISHED TITLES

Ramón María del Valle Inclán, *Savage Comedies*
Translated and edited by Christopher Colbath and Luis M. González

Michel-Jean Sedaine, *Le Philosophe sans le savoir*
Translated by Derek Connon

In Defence of Women
Translated by Joanna M. Barker

Hugo van Hofmannsthal, *The Incorruptible Servant*
Translated by Alexander Stillmark

Goethe, *The Natural Daughter* & Schiller, *The Bride of Messina*
Translated by F. J. Lamport

Georg Kaiser, *After Expressionism: Five Plays*
Translated by Fred Bridgham

texts.mhra.org.uk

To sign up to the series mailing list, email newtranslations@mhra.org.uk

www.ingramcontent.com/pod-product-compliance
Lightning Source LLC
Chambersburg PA
CBHW070615170426
43200CB00012B/2699